Editor
Lorin E. Klistoff, M.A.

Managing Editor
Karen J. Goldfluss, M.S. E.d.

Cover Artist
Tony Carrillo

Creative Director
Karen J. Goldfluss, M.S. Ed.

Art Production Manager
Kevin Barnes

Art Coordinator
Renée Christine Yates

Imaging
Leonard P. Swierski

Publisher

Mary D. Smith, M.S. Ed.

Author

Alan Horsfield

Teacher Created Resources, Inc.
6421 Industry Way
Westminster, CA 92683
www.teachercreated.com

ISBN: 978-1-4206-8047-8

© 2007 Teacher Created Resources, Inc.
Made in U.S.A.

Strategies in This Book

This book is intended to help students develop successful strategies for reading comprehension. The students accomplish this by reading passages and articles and then answering a variety of questions using a specific strategy. When the student completes the exercises, he or she will have practiced a strategy and worked through a number of question types from a variety of texts.

Rather than give a range of strategies for each passage, the focus will be on developing the student's skill in applying one particular strategy. The book is structured so that if a student is having difficulty in one area, he or she can concentrate on a strategy that will help improve comprehension. The strategies included in this book are listed below.

STRATEGIES

Each new section provides information on what is required for the particular strategy being practiced. The first introduction page in each section is intended to lead the student through a given strategy. The answers for all questions are provided at the back of the book.

Text Types

In addition to providing strategy practice, this book also offers a range of text types so the student will feel confident in a variety of situations. Text types are usually broken into two broad categories. Within each group are a number of choices—some are listed below.

- *Literary texts*—include narratives (novels/stories), poetry, and scripts (drama)

- *Factual texts*—include explanations, expositions, information reports, recounts, and procedures

As one can see, the list is quite long. It is important that students develop comprehension skills from a variety of text types.

(*Note to Teacher:* In this book, on a number of occasions, the passages are reused. This is done to demonstrate that a variety of comprehension strategies can be applied to the same piece of writing. Comprehension skills are interdependent.)

Question Types

Question types included in this book are as follows:

- true/false responses
- short answers
- matching exercises
- sequencing
- giving reasons
- language knowledge
- predicting skills
- inferring skills
- recognizing "audience"
- recognizing purpose
- multiple-choice responses
- full sentence answers
- sentence completion
- open-ended responses
- cloze exercises
- giving opinions and justifying them
- labelling skills
- interpreting data
- discussing theme/plot
- understanding shades of meaning

Standards

The standards and benchmarks that are listed on page 5 will be met or reinforced by completing the practice pages included in this book. These standards and benchmarks are similar to the ones required by your state and school district. The standards and benchmarks are taken from *A Compendium of Standards and Benchmarks for K–12 Education* (Copyright 2004 McREL, www.mcrel.org/standards-benchmarks) Language Arts (Grades 6–8). They are displayed in a simple-to-read reference chart. The chart shows the pages to which the standard and benchmarks specifically refer.

Graphic Organizers

At the end of the book, there are a variety of graphic organizers to help your students organize their ideas and concepts when reading a certain passage and working on a certain strategy. Learners of all kinds will be able to visualize their information and ideas when familiar with graphic organizers. Students will be better able to access, understand, organize, and present information.

REFERENCE CHART

Standard: Uses the general skills and strategies of the writing process	
Benchmark: Writes in response to literature	Pages 7–65

Standard: Uses the stylistic and rhetorical aspects of writing	
Benchmark: Uses descriptive language that clarifies and enhances ideas	Pages 47–49
Benchmark: Uses paragraph form in writing	Pages 44–46
Benchmark: Uses a variety of sentence structures in writing	Pages 7–65

Standard: Uses grammatical and mechanical conventions in written compositions	
Benchmark: Uses nouns in written compositions	Page 9
Benchmark: Uses verbs in written compositions	Page 9
Benchmark: Uses adjectives in written compositions	Page 9
Benchmark: Uses adverbs in written compositions	Page 9
Benchmark: Uses prepositions and coordinating conjuctions in written compositions	Page 9
Benchmark: Uses conventions of spelling in written compositions	Pages 7–65
Benchmark: Uses conventions of capitalization in written compositions	Pages 7–65
Benchmark: Uses conventions of punctuation in written compositions	Pages 7–65

Standard: Gathers and uses information for research purposes	
Benchmark: Gathers data for research topics from interviews	Page 27
Benchmark: Uses a variety of resource materials to gather information for research topics (e.g., magazines, newspapers, dictionaries, schedules, journals, phone directories, globes, atlases, almanacs, technological sources)	Pages 45, 77
Benchmark: Organizes information and ideas from multiple sources in systematic ways	Pages 77–80

Standard: Uses the general skills and strategies of the reading process	
Benchmark: Establishes and adjusts purposes for reading	Pages 7–65
Benchmark: Uses a variety of strategies to extend reading vocabulary	Pages 7–65
Benchmark: Uses specific strategies to clear up confusing parts of a text	Pages 7–65
Benchmark: Understands specific devices an author uses to accomplish his or her purpose	Pages 26, 47–49
Benchmark: Reflects on what has been learned after reading and formulates ideas, opinions, and personal responses to texts	Pages 7, 20, 31, 44

Standard: Uses reading skills and strategies to understand and interpret a variety of literary texts	
Benchmark: Uses reading skills and strategies to understand and interpret a variety of literary passages and texts	Pages 9, 10, 15, 19–26, 29–31, 36, 44, 46, 50
Benchmark: Understands complex elements of plot development	Pages 9, 10, 15, 19–26, 29–31 36, 44, 46, 50
Benchmark: Understands elements of character development	Pages 9, 10, 15, 19–26, 29–31, 36, 44, 46, 50
Benchmark: Understands the effects of an author's style on the reader	Pages 47–49
Benchmark: Understands inferred and recurring themes in literary works	Page 21
Benchmark: Makes connections between the motives of characters or the causes for complex events in texts and those in his or her own life	Pages 20, 31, 44

Standard: Uses reading skills and strategies to understand and interpret a variety of informational texts	
Benchmark: Uses reading skills and strategies to understand a variety of informational texts	Pages 7, 8, 11–14, 16–18, 27, 28, 32–35, 37–43, 45–47, 49–59, 61–65
Benchmark: Summarizes and paraphrases information in texts	Pages 17, 18
Benchmark: Uses new information to adjust and extend personal knowledge base	Pages 7, 8, 11–14, 16–18, 27, 28, 32–35, 37–43, 45–47, 49–59, 61–65
Benchmark: Draws conclusions and makes inferences based on explicit and implicit information in texts	Pages 8, 13, 27, 33–36
Benchmark: Differentiates between fact and opinion in informational texts	Pages 50–52

*All standards listed above are from *A Compendium of Standards and Benchmarks for K–12 Education* (Copyright 2004 McREL, www.mcrel.org/standards-benchmarks) Language Arts (Grades 6–8).

Name: _____   Date: _____

OVERVIEW

A **text** is any meaningful written message. It is communication. In writing, we can create texts. By reading and listening, we can understand and interpret texts.

Text types are often called genres. Text types can be classified in a number of ways. The following classification has been adapted from *Basic Primary Grammar* by P. Walker (Pascal Press, 1996 Edition). Text types are often broadly classified into two basic types: literary and factual.

Literary texts

Narratives	Drama	Poetry

Examples

novels stories myths/legends science fiction fantasy fables jokes	stage plays film scripts radio scripts	limericks lyrics sonnets nonsense rhymes poems songs jingles

Text types can overlap. For example, a stage play may be written in verse.
Try these questions.

1. Name a famous playwright who wrote plays in verse. _____

2. In which column would you put **comics**? _____

3. What is your reason? _____

Factual texts

Discussions	Explanations	Expositions	Information Reports	Procedures	Recounts

Examples

debates
talk radio
  discussions
	text books
	scientific writing
	spoken
	  presentations
		advertisements
		lectures
		editorials
		speeches
		letters to
		  editors
		newspaper
		  cartoons
			documentaries
			announcements
			reference
			  books
			guide books
				instructions
				directions
				recipes
				tables of events
					diaries
					newspaper
					  reports
					historical reports
					letters
					logs
					timelines

No doubt more examples of text types can be added to this list.

Factual text types can overlap too. An historical recount may be presented as a TV play.

Interpreting data is an important skill in modern society. Data may include graphs, timetables, flow charts, maps, and labeled diagrams.

Try these questions.

4. Name a famous writer of a diary. _____

5. In which column would you put postcards? _____

6. What is your reason? _____

7. In what group would you put a poster for a Disney film? _____

8. What is your reason? _____

INTRODUCTION

In comprehension exercises, you will see many different types of questions. These are used to see just how well you comprehend what you have read.

- Questions that want you to find information may begin with *how, when, where,* or *what.* Sometimes you will be asked to give names, make lists, or even label diagrams.
- Questions that want you to give a reason will often begin with *why.*
- Some questions may ask you to give an opinion. For these questions you need to have your own ideas and you should answer in your own words based upon information available or your understanding of a topic. For these questions, there is really no right or wrong answer as long as you can give an adequate reason.
- Other questions may ask you to search and find information in the text, especially in factual texts.

Read the following excerpt and answer the questions.

What do you really understand about hypnotism? More to the point, what do you believe?

Have you ever seen a hypnotist on television, making people quack like ducks or sing like Elvis, and wondered, "Can hypnotists really make you do something you wouldn't normally do?" or "Can a hypnotist really control your mind?" Well, psychologists have the answer.

Based upon what they have seen on television, at the movies, and during stage shows which feature hypnosis, many believe that hypnosis can be used to control people without their consent. It has been reported that, last century, people who committed crimes, supposedly under the influence of an unscrupulous hypnotist, were not legally responsible for their actions.

Recent research by psychologists tells us that a response to hypnotic suggestion is not due to the powers of the hypnotist, but to the talent and willingness of the hypnotized person—the volunteer.

1. *What* does the author suggest is the truth behind hypnotism? (full sentence answer)

_____.

2. Draw a line to *match* each sentence beginning with its correct ending.

TV show volunteers   has cast doubt on the popularly held beliefs.

Research by psychologists   are often willing to be hypnotized.

Hypnotists   are generally believed to have special powers.

3. *True or False:* Hypnotists make people commit crimes. ☐ True ☐ False (Check one box.)

4. *Sentence completion:* A response to hypnotic suggestion is due to _____

_____.

5. *Opinion:* Do you think people should be hypnotized to act in an embarrassing way? _____

What is your reason? _____

_____

Name: _____   Date: _____

FREEFLYERS: MODERN SKYDIVERS

Imagine falling toward the planet Earth at a terrifying 300 kilometers per hour. You started your fall from over four kilometers above the Earth. And you have less than one minute before you pull your parachute cord. You are falling so fast that just turning your head can send you off in a different direction. This is the wild side of a sport that has not found its limits— freeflying.

Freeflying is a variation on the more **traditional** skydiving. Skydivers were groups of jumpers who created magnificent, often very difficult maneuvers in free fall. With skydiving, all the jumpers are travelling at the same speed in the same arena of activity. They create formations and movements that make the onlookers gape in awe.

Even experienced skydivers watch the antics of freeflyers in amazement. The skill and control to be a freeflyer leaves many formation flyers shaking their heads.

Freeflyers, as the name suggests, do not hang around in crowds. Freeflyers enjoy the more spontaneous thrill of doing their own thing.

The wildest trip for a freeflyer is falling "head down." You are heading straight to Earth headfirst! Falling "head first" requires a great deal of control—and nerve. The small surface presented to the air means that not only do you travel faster but the slightest movement has a greater effect on your direction.

Even the gear of freeflyers is more **outrageous**. They wear the zaniest jumpsuits, outlandish helmets, and smaller parachutes. In fact, their parachutes are about one quarter the size of the traditional skydivers' parachutes, which means they surf to the ground at about sixty kilometers per hour.

It is only in the last few years that freeflying has gained any real public acceptance.

---

1. *Opinion:* Which of the two activities—skydiving or freeflying— do you think would be the most

   dangerous? _____ Briefly give your reason. _____

Search and find: Write short answers (one or two words) for questions 2 through 4.

2. How fast do freeflyers fall before they use their chute? _____

3. How long do freeflyers drop before pulling the cord? _____

4. What activity are skydivers most interested in? _____

5. *True or False:* Most people find skydiving a spectacular sport. ☐ True ☐ False (Check one.)

6. *Inferring:* Freeflyers could best be described as (impudent   disorganized   daring). (Circle one.)

7. *Reasoning:* Skydiving requires more cooperation of participants than freeflying does because

   _____ .

8. *Language:* The word "outrageous" could best be replaced by (shocking   sensational). (Circle one.)

9. *Language:* Which of the following words is closest in meaning to the word "traditional," as used in

   the passage?   (historical   reliable   conventional   cautious)   (Circle one answer.)

10. *Audience:* This passage would most likely be found in a manual teaching people how to freefly.

    ☐ True   ☐ False

Name: _____ Date: _____

CLOZE EXERCISES

Cloze exercises can have a variety of purposes. They can test your understanding of grammatical features of language. They can test your word knowledge, or they can test your comprehension of an extract. In cloze exercises, you have to select the best word to fill (close) the space. To do cloze exercises well, you should read the title of the excerpt, if there is one, the whole excerpt, and look at any graphics before beginning. When you have completed the exercise, read it through again, from the beginning, to ensure it makes sense. It can help to mouth the words as you read them.

Read these excerpts and answer the questions. This is a grammar/spelling-type exercise. (Circle the correct letter—don't write in the spaces.)

As he ran for the school bus he felt great, not just because he was going home after a difficult day, _____(1)_____ because the run itself was exhilarating. The driver smiled as he jumped to the steps just as the door closed and he said, "Made it!"

He was surprised when she replied. "You look as if you just escaped _____(2)_____ an angry mob."

People don't seem to make light conversation anymore, he thought. Haven't got the time, he supposed. Or just too preoccupied to be friendly. His smile widened as the bus pulled into the line of traffic.

Things _____(3)_____ looking better already.

1. (A) or
(B) but
(C) and
(D) yet

2. (A) off
(B) into
(C) from
(D) away

3. (A) is
(B) are
(C) was
(D) were

This time consider the meanings of the words and the context in which they are used. Read the excerpt from *Streetscape* by Ian Steep.

At the outdoor cafe people sat _____(4)_____ over small tables to chat, or stretched back and reading newspapers; the winter sunshine was more important than their coffee and cakes.

It was already late morning and Michael was hungry. He kept moving to _____(5)_____ suspicion, walking slowly past shop windows examining the _____(6)_____. Harry's cafe was reflected in the glass. A couple of girls Michael knew had settled themselves on a planter box near the tables, and were **slyly** observing the customers.

A taxi turned the corner and pulled into the curb. A smartly dressed woman reached forward to pay the driver then she pushed open the taxi door. As she stepped onto the pavement the girls made their _____(7)_____. As carelessly as hurried shoppers, as carefully as jewel thieves, they moved towards the woman. It was all over before anyone saw what had happened.

4. (A) hurled
(B) huddled
(C) stranded
(D) crowded

5. (A) avoid
(B) dodge
(C) baffle
(D) report

6. (A) scene
(B) exhibit
(C) displays
(D) evidence

7. (A) bid
(B) move
(C) action
(D) proposal

8. The word "slyly" means to act (Check one answer.)

☐ in a criminal manner. ☐ with stealth. ☐ slowly.

Name: _____   Date: _____

CIRCLES

Read the passage from William Taylor's book *Circles* and answer the multiple-choice questions. Circle one letter for questions 1 through 4. Question 5 is a sequencing question. (**Note:** In passages where the name of the storyteller is not known, he or she is often referred to as the narrator.)

My mother died of sick madness. She died of this sick madness and of grief and fear. She died in a strange and alien place, so far from what she thought of as home, a home she would never, ever see again.

If a story may be said to have a beginning, this is the beginning of mine. In truth, I know, the story of no one really does have a beginning. There must always be something that has just gone on before and there were, naturally, a lot of somethings that happened before my mother's death that indeed led to that cursed and dreadful moment. It is true, though, that the dying of the poor, sad woman I loved so dearly really did provide the marker, the turning point to my subsequent existence.

It was fifty years ago to the day, the day on which I choose to begin to write these words, fifty years ago that my father, my brother, and I dug her grave,

dressed Mother in her own good gown, wrapped her remains, poor thin little soul she had become, in the linen that had once been her mother's, and laid her to rest among those trees. At rest in those trees, beneath the trees she had so greatly feared. She rests there today, a scant half mile from where I sit writing these words, words that I write surrounded by a comfort and splendor that she never experienced and of which, likely, simple soul, she never dreamed.

Today I pushed my way through the under-growth, doing my best to follow the ill-formed track to the spot beneath the giant rimu tree where a slab of marble says: "Elizabeth Costello 1840–1876 and John Costello 1839–1876." My father, foolish man, lost spirit, survived his wife by no more than a handful of hours. Robert and I dug his grave and then we left this place with, in reality, little hope of ever seeing it again.

---

1. Elizabeth Costello could best be described as living

(A) a life of sorrow and desperation.

(B) a simple and bountiful country life.

(C) surrounded by comfort and splendor.

(D) in the one place for the whole of her life.

2. Fifty years before the narrator started writing,

(A) he left home, never expecting to return.

(B) his brother was buried under the trees.

(C) his parents arrived in a strange and alien land.

(D) he revisited his parents' graves for the first time.

3. The narrator's return to his parents' graves had been

(A) planned well in advance.

(B) undertaken many times.

(C) something he'd thought he couldn't do.

(D) in the company of his brother.

4. This passage, most likely, originally came from

(A) a manual.

(B) an historical recount.

(C) a teenagers' magazine.

(D) a review.

5. Write the numbers 1 through 4 in the boxes to show the <u>sequence</u> of events in the passage.

☐ John Costello dies.

☐ The narrator began his writing.

☐ The sons dig their mother's grave.

☐ Elizabeth Costello leaves her childhood home.

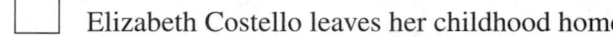

Name: _____   Date: _____

INTRODUCTION

When **finding facts**, you will often be asked questions beginning with *who, when, where, what,* and *how,* and sometimes *why.* You will be asked to search for answers to questions that help you understand the time (when) and place (where) of the action in the excerpt, as well as who or what is involved. *Which* may also be used. Sometimes you will be asked to give names or make lists.

You will be expected to find facts in both factual materials and narratives (stories). In factual material, important points may be introduced with bullet points (•).

Many exercises in this part of the book are based upon factual writing. "Polar Ice," an excerpt from *The Earth* by Q. L. Pearce, is a good place to start looking for facts. Generally, you should answer with full sentence answers unless asked to do otherwise. Full sentence answers help you to focus on what the question is actually asking.

Now read the excerpt.

POLAR ICE

We have all seen those beautiful documentaries on television which provide viewers with brilliant pictures of the South Polar region—stark white landscapes and seascapes against a backdrop of crisp blue skies. The Antarctic is a special place of ice and snow. It is the ice and snow that makes it so spectacular.

When salt water freezes, it is called pack ice. The cold winds of the polar regions chill the sea water until it forms plates of ice crystals called frazel ice. The thin frazel ice sheets on the surface are usually broken up by water movement into large irregular disks, or pancake ice. Further freezing creates a solid slab called an ice floe. New ice floes are two to three meters thick. If they do not melt away in summer, they refreeze in winter, becoming even thicker. Seas of pack ice widen in winter and recede in summer, but the polar regions have huge areas of permanent pack ice. Special ships, called ice breakers, can often plow through these frozen seas.

In the Antarctic, layers of snow on land are compressed into huge rivers of ice. These rivers of ice, glaciers, flow towards the sea at speeds from a few centimeters to a few meters per day, but this can vary widely. At the sea, chunks of glacial ice break off into the water. This is called calving. The chunk of ice, or iceberg, floats with only one tenth of its mass above the surface, and may travel great distances. In the Antarctic, icebergs break off from the iceshelf and are often flatter, wider, and more numerous than Arctic icebergs.

The tallest iceberg ever sighted was near Greenland, with almost 170 meters showing above water. The biggest iceberg was an Antarctic iceberg which covered an area the size of Belgium.

---

1. <u>What</u> is another name for pack ice? (short answer) _____

2. <u>Where</u> are the most icebergs found? (full sentence answer) _____

   _____.

3. <u>What</u> fraction of an iceberg is below the water line? _____

4. Many of the glaciers of the Antarctic region end up as

   (A) frazel ice.

   (B) ice floes.

   (C) pack ice.

   (D) icebergs.

5. Select the correct fact to complete this sentence. Ships, called icebreakers, are used to

   ☐ smash icebergs.   ☐ plow through pack ice.   ☐ break chunks off icebergs.

6. By late summer, all Antarctic ice has melted.   ☐ True   ☐ False

FINDING THE FACTS

MYSTERY IN MANDURAH

by Jill Burgess

In March 1969, a tragedy struck when local fishermen Hugh Gill and Bevan Hahn went fishing for crayfish and were never seen again.

Resident Jim Spice could recall the day he went to meet Gill's vessel, the *Avaneta*, at the government jetty. But it was an appointment **she** did not keep.

Gill, 62, and Hahn, 33, were last seen shifting craypots more than 36 km off Halls Head, but an intensive search by fishermen and a coastal sweep by a **flotilla** of yachts returning from Bunbury failed to turn up any clues.

The weather was rough and the 22-year-old boat, previously wrecked on the entrance bar, should not have been rebuilt and certainly not have put to sea in the condition it was in.

Later, fisherman Ray Brennan discovered a number of craypots, floats, and ropes adrift in the general area of the *Avaneta*'s last sighting.

The floats were clearly marked with the vessel's number and an echo sounder revealed an object the size of the missing vessel 40 m down on the ocean bed.

Convinced it was *Avaneta*, Brennan and others marked the spot and spent precious time needed to prepare for the crayfish season guiding police and divers to the spot.

But the search was called off when police claimed their divers were not equipped to do deep dives.

Later in the year, a row was brewing as fishermen and residents claimed police were reluctant to follow a lead which could solve the disappearance.

There were conflicting opinions as to why specialist help was not obtained and the site investigated further.

According to reports, the marker flag was moved when the dive was abandoned and the spot could not later be identified.

A second theory blamed the recent Meekering earthquake which caused tremors which set the flag adrift and shifted the vessel on the ocean bed.

The marker was eventually found miles away.

Although air, sea, and land searches revealed few answers, fishermen were on the lookout for several weeks.

But the only clue ever to come to light was Gill's fishing box, found on the beach.

The *Avaneta* had a small cabin and craypots were stacked in the stern.

Jim Spice believed an unexpected wave could have struck the *Avaneta*, tossing the stern into the air and sending the craypots sliding down the deck to lodge against the cabin door.

Had the two men been in the cabin at the time, they would have been trapped as the boat capsized or was swamped.

Others maintain the *Avaneta* may have been swamped by a huge wave and gone to the bottom.

Whatever happened to the *Avaneta* and her crew is a mystery unlikely ever to be solved.

---

1. If Ray Brennan hadn't been assisting police, he would have been _____

_____.

2. In the second paragraph (commencing "Resident Jim Spice . . ."), the word "she" refers to _____.

3. Jim Spice believes the loss of the *Avaneta* was the result of

   (A) rough weather.   (C) poor repairs to the damaged vessel after it was wrecked.

   (B) the Meekering earthquake.   (D) an unexpected wave swamping the boat.

4. On information provided in the report, what would you conclude happened to the *Avaneta*?

_____

5. In the report a "flotilla" is a (A) sea patrol.   (B) small fleet.   (C) commander.   (D) naval force.

6. Why did the residents of Mandurah become upset with the police?

_____

THE TREE OF LIFE

If there is one thing that really comes to mind when the words, "South Pacific," are spoken, then it must be palms, especially coconut palms. We all have images of tall coconut palms leaning gracefully over sandy coral beaches. But the coconut tree is more than a beautiful palm that is the central feature of picture postcards purchased by tourists.

To people of the South Pacific the coconut tree is also known as the "Tree of Life." It owes this name to the wide variety of products which the coconut palm provides from its various parts. From the leaves down to its roots it plays a significant part in the life of many island people. Name it, the coconut provides it—food, shelter, or fuel—as well as income from exports.

Leaves. Coconut leaves produce good quality paper pulp, midrib brooms, hats and mats, fruit trays, wastebaskets, placemats, and bags.

Coconuts (fruit). Flesh and water (often called the milk) from the young, green coconut can be taken as a health food and drink. It is also used as a main ingredient for salads and other delicacies.

Husks. Coconut husks contain 10% bristle fiber, 20% mattress filling, and 70% coir. Often the husk is thrown away, but it can be used to produce a wide variety of useful products such as ropes, mats, fishing nets, household wall and floor coverings.

Water. Coconut water can be used in the production of vinegar and wine, and is also used to treat a number of medical disorders.

Flesh. The white coconut flesh is a good source of protein, coconut oil, coconut flour, shredded coconut, coconut chips, and feed for animals.

Coconut shell. The shell can be used to make attractive handicrafts, novelty items, charcoal briquettes for cooking, and high quality industrial carbons.

Trunk. The trunk of the coconut tree is a hardy and durable wood. It is used to make furniture. Paper pulp can also be made from the trunk.

Roots. Medicines, beverage extracts, and dyes are obtained from the roots.

The English oak, the Lebanon cedar, or the Australian gum tree all have a place in history, but the coconut palm is the only true "Tree of Life."

---

1. What are the four useful parts of the fruit of the coconut palm?

a. _____ b. _____ c. _____ d. _____

2. How do tourists react to coconut palms? _____

Basket

3. Why do many South Pacific people call the coconut palm the "Tree of Life"?

_____

Coconut oil

Fresh coconut

Answer *True* or *False* to the facts expressed in Questions 4, 5, and 6.

4. Medicines can be produced from the leaves. _____

5. The wood of the coconut palm has limited use in building. _____

Mosquito coil

6. Palm leaves can be used in paper making. _____

Handicraft

7. In your own words, explain the meaning of the word "durable." _____

_____

8. The South Pacific people regard the coconut palm as (Check one box.)

☐ a visual pollution of coral beaches.

☐ a tree that is in oversupply.

☐ a tree of little local importance.

☐ one of the world's great trees.

SOAP

Soap

Flooring

9. In your opinion, what part of the coconut palm is most useful? _____

Name: _____   Date: _____

THE TOMMY TYCHO STORY
by Tommy Tycho

Since I was born, I have been surrounded by music. Not just any music, but the right kind of music.

It may seem odd to say that, but hearing good music played well by a big ensemble is something that a lot of people no longer experience or appreciate. Most people are **musically illiterate** simply because they have never been exposed to good music. Many people are unfamiliar with the sound of a symphony orchestra, which to me is the biggest instrument in the world. They hear orchestra music underscoring ads and films; they hear a trio and think of it as a band. To hear a full symphony orchestra on stage and to feel the power of the sound—it is like a tidal wave. It is an amazing experience and it is one that I was lucky enough to grow up with.

My mother was a **celebrated** soprano. Her name was Helen Tehel. She had been a member of the Vienna State Opera and the Budapest State Opera before her marriage, and as a baby I was dragged along to concerts, the opera, and operetta stages. I was spoiled rotten, surrounded not necessarily by classical music but good, high-quality music played well.

My mother was the sixteenth child in her family. She was the youngest and by the time she was born, her oldest sister also had a child with whom she shared a crib.

Because I lost my father when I was very young, I do not remember much about him. What I do know is largely what I have been told by my mother. I resemble him in many ways. He was evidently a very serious man, bordering on melancholy. I seem to have inherited something of that from him. Fortunately, I inherited far more of my mother's vitality and energy—a real show business personality.

1. This type of writing could best be described as _____ .

2. A person who is "musically illiterate" would, most likely, be a person who
   (A) could not play any musical instrument.
   (B) has inherited their ability from their parents.
   (C) had only a limited variety of musical experiences.
   (D) had never been to a performance of a symphony orchestra.

3. Titles guide the reader to important facts. Another good title for this excerpt would be:
   (A) Growing Up with Music
   (B) An Amazing Experience
   (C) Life in a Large Family
   (D) Following in My Father's Footsteps

4. Tommy Tycho's mother was very indulgent of him. ☐ True ☐ False

5. Full orchestras are usually used to provide music for ads. ☐ True ☐ False

6. How do you think Tommy Tycho would describe his childhood? _____

7. In the extract, the word "celebrated" means
   ☐ thrilling.   ☐ distinguished.
   ☐ remarkable.   ☐ honored.

8. From this excerpt, how would you predict Tommy Tycho's life turned out?

_____

9. Where do you think Tommy Tycho was born? _____

Name: _____   Date: _____

NIGHT OF THE MUTTONBIRDS

The story *Night of the Muttonbirds* by Mary Small is an example of <u>realistic writing</u>. It is based upon her real-life experiences, so it is a good book for finding facts that are not from factual writing.

Matthew shifted restlessly in his chair and glanced up at the schoolroom clock on the wall opposite. Ten-thirty already! What had happened? Had something gone wrong? Today was mail day but the plane was later than usual, and on this of all days when his grandmother, Annie, was returning from the hospital in Tasmania. In nervous anticipation he sat staring out of the window, chewing his fingernails, listening, waiting.

"Matthew!" Mr. Trent's voice was sharp. It was difficult to keep this eleven-year-old occupied in such a small class of children—all of different ages.

Matthew glanced at him in exasperation, sighed and made a half-hearted attempt to concentrate on the subject in front of him. Then, to his enormous relief, he heard it, at first indistinct but unmistakable. The low steady drone of an aircraft approaching. He stood up pushing his books aside.

"Matthew! Sit down!"

"It's coming," said Matthew. "The plane, I mean. Mr. Greg's coming."

All the children sitting around the long table in the school classroom looked up.

Matthew was already halfway to the open door, his face anxious.

"Can I come too?" asked Shelley, his nine-year-old sister.

"And me too?" piped up his brother, five-year-old Clinton, his green smock splattered with bright colors from the dripping paint pots on his painting easel.

Deborah stood up. "I want to see Grannie," she said.

"And me!" cried Jim, sliding backwards off his chair.

"Sit down!" said Mr. Trent crossly. "No, not you, Matthew. I promised you could come but remember it's on the condition you work through your lunch hour." With almost half the class grandchildren of old Annie, he had to be strict. "Shelley, are you listening? I'm leaving you in charge. There'll be no fooling around while I'm away."

1. Name the main character in the excerpt. _____

2. What was Shelley's relationship to Clinton? Clinton was

☐ an older sister. ☐ a younger sister. ☐ a younger brother. ☐ the only brother.

3. What was causing Matthew to be nervous?

☐ The late arrival of the plane. ☐ The return of his grandmother.

☐ Leaving Shelley in charge of the class. ☐ Not being able to finish his work on time.

4. Which word would best describe Mr. Trent's behavior as the plane approached? (Circle one answer.)

fearful   relaxed   agitated   pleased   distraught

5. Mr. Trent found his class difficult to control because

(A) Matthew wouldn't listen.   (B) the students were all different ages.

(C) the school was so small.   (D) Annie was returning to Tasmania.

6. Shelley has to pick up the paint from the floor.   ☐ True   ☐ False

7. Mr. Greg was most likely to be _____ .

8. Who spoke the words, "Matthew! Sit down!"? _____

OUR NEIGHBOR IN SPACE

from the Marlin Space Mission website

Mars is famous for its color, its volcanoes, and its sand dunes. Its polar regions are also of interest to scientists. The *Mars Global Surveyor* orbited Mars and photographed and sent back information to Earth on the North Pole of Mars.

The northern spring in Mars begins in mid-July. With the arrival of spring there is the annual shrinkage of the northern polar ice cap. When sunlight begins to shine on the northern ice cap, the frost and ice begin their retreat.

But this is not the normal Earth-like ice and snow that melts to become water. Mars' ice and snow are formed from carbon dioxide and when they melt they don't turn into a liquid—they change directly from a solid to a gas. And when this happens the surface of Mars is quickly revealed.

What was photographed in July 1998 was a view of the Martian sand dunes. Just a few months earlier they were obscured by frost, thick clouds, and the Martian night—a bit like the night at Earth's Poles.

This vast sea of sand dunes surround the North Pole. They were first seen by *Viking 2 Orbiter* in 1976. The size and shape of the crescent dunes are similar to sand dunes found in many desert regions on Earth, which are formed when the wind persistently comes from the one direction.

As spring progresses, the sky above the Martian dunes clears. Northern summer begins early in January.

Because it was in polar orbit, *Mars Global Orbiter* had many opportunities to photograph the region and collect important information on the changes that take place over a number of Martian seasons.

---

1. What is this passage about? _____

_____.

2. Write letters (a, b, or c) in the brackets to match the correct sentence beginning.

   (a) With the advent of spring   (   ) sunlight begins to shine on the ice cap.

   (b) By late January   (   ) sand dunes are concealed under a frost cover.

   (c) Before July   (   ) the ice cap has shrunk.

3. The photographs of Mars were taken by a passing spacecraft.   ☐ True   ☐ False

4. The North Pole of Mars is surrounded by a vast ocean.   ☐ True   ☐ False

5. How does the snow and ice on Mars differ from snow and ice on Earth? _____

_____

6. Why are the Martian sand dunes crescent shaped? _____

_____

7. The *Mars Global Orbiter's* mission was to

   (A) take photos of the northern polar ice cap only.

   (B) collect information about the seasons on Mars.

   (C) gather samples from the Martian sand dunes.

   (D) find landing sites for a scientific mission.

Name: _____   Date: _____

INTRODUCTION

When studying texts, you will often be asked to **find the main idea**. In paragraphs, the main idea is often the same as the topic sentence. It is the most important piece of information for the reader. All other sentences in the paragraph add to the meaning of the topic sentence. They are often called the supporting details. (See Understanding Paragraphs, page 44.)

The topic sentence is often the first sentence, but it can come in the middle of the paragraph or at the end. If it is quite long, it may sometimes contain more information than just the main idea.

In longer works, we often talk about the theme, or central idea. Titles and headings often give a clue about the main idea in books or in chapters. If we look at the extract, "Native Animals as Pets" from *Pets, the Law and You in NSW*, by Karen Dunn, we can use it to start finding the main idea.

NATIVE ANIMALS AS PETS

Pets play an important role in our society (*main idea/topic sentence*). They provide us with companionship, love and affection, benefits to our health, and sometimes even security (*supporting detail*). In order to care for our pets in the best way possible, it is important to know about the laws affecting us and our animals (*supporting detail*).

The Australian *National Parks and Wildlife Act 1974* contains regulations about the keeping of native animals as pets. Under the act it is an offense to buy, sell, or possess protected fauna unless you have the appropriate license. The penalty is $2,000 or imprisonment for six months.

It is possible to obtain a license from the National Parks and Wildlife Service to keep native birds and some species of reptiles. The department will only give licenses for the keeping of two types of mammals—the spinifex hopping mouse and the plains rat—and will not give licenses to keep native amphibians.

The penalty for keeping endangered fauna is a fine of $4,000 or imprisonment for 12 months. The penalty for keeping marine mammals and threatened native fauna is a $10,000 fine or imprisonment for two years. As the regulations are constantly changing, before contemplating obtaining any sort of native animal, first check with the Service. Humane Society International does not encourage the keeping of any native animals as pets.

If you find an injured native animal or bird, contact the Wildlife Information and Rescue Service (WIRES). WIRES has experienced people to nurse sick and injured animals back to health. They have special licenses which allow them to care for animals that are otherwise illegal to keep.

---

1. The main idea in the second paragraph ("The Australian *National* . . .") centers on
   - (A) buying and selling protected fauna.
   - (B) the fines for keeping native animals.
   - (C) the provisions of the *National Parks and Wildlife Act 1974*.
   - (D) why people should get a license to keep native animals.

2. What is the main idea in the third paragraph?
   - (A) keeping amphibians
   - (B) two special Australian mammals
   - (C) rules for keeping birds
   - (D) obtaining licenses

3. It is important for anyone who finds an injured native animal to nurse it back to health.

   ☐ True   ☐ False

4. Which one of the following is a good alternate heading for this excerpt? (Circle one answer.)

   People Need Pets   Native Fauna Regulations   Saving Our Wildlife

5. What <u>theme</u> is developed in the text? _____

---

* FINDING THE MAIN IDEA *

EARTH FIRST
by David Bowden & Jenny Dibley

Technology vs. the Environment

In developed countries, consumption is viewed as essential for economic growth. In recent decades, however, concern has grown about the increasing number of people consuming finite resources at an alarming rate.

People in developed countries consume far more resources per person than those in developing countries. Developed countries have the power to lead the world toward environmental **consumerism** because they use the most resources.

Sophisticated packaging and storage, such as refrigeration, is a luxury that consumers in developed countries take for granted. In many parts of the world where refrigeration is either unavailable or too expensive, fresh food is purchased daily from open-air markets.

These markets make little impact upon the environment. They do not use energy to store food and because they mostly operate during daylight hours, no electricity is used for lighting. Packaging is mostly unnecessary, and when needed, is often made from biodegradable vegetable matter.

These markets still exist in many parts of the developed world, but are an alternative form of shopping. Even in developing countries, shops are fast becoming the primary outlets for consumers.

Commercial packaging is becoming as much a part of consumption in developing countries as it is in developed countries. Plastic bags, aluminium drink cans, cardboard cartons, and polystyrene hamburger containers are now swept into rubbish piles along with banana leaves which are a more traditional form of packaging. In most cases, it all ends up at the local dump and is not recycled.

Many people are starting to notice the impact of consumerism on the environment. It is affecting not only the planet, but also our health. Some scientists think that the greenhouse effect and depletion of the ozone layer have increased due to the production, use, and disposal of many of the products we use.

1. What is the main idea in the first paragraph?_____

_____

2. The author considers packaging and refrigeration to be (luxuries   necessities   progress). (Circle one.)

3. What is meant by the word "consumerism"? _____

_____

4. Explain the main idea of paragraph 6. _____

_____

5. Paragraph 5 tells us that the trend towards open-air markets in developing countries is

(increasing   declining   stable). (Circle one answer.)

6. When did people start becoming concerned about how resources were being consumed?

_____

7. What do you think is the main point of the passage? _____

_____

LAND OF THE RIPPLING GOLD

by Una Clarke

Read this passage from *Land of the Rippling Gold* by Una Clarke and answer the questions.

Wendy blamed herself for the accident. If she hadn't been daydreaming out of the opposite window, she might have seen the stump and yelled in time for her father to turn the wheel. There wasn't another stump or tree on the roadside for miles. Besides, it was her fault they were even there, and now her mother sat there injured.

Two weeks had passed since her leg was gouged by Marjorie's bike. Christmas had come and gone. The slight wound had seemed to be healing, then suddenly swelled up in a shiny painful lump, upsetting her mother. Having suffered so dreadfully with a poisoned leg herself, and fearing for her child, she had insisted on consulting the doctor in the next town that very day. Her father, reluctant to lose a day's work, argued that a good **poulticing** would fix it. Edie had flared up at that, saying his family had said the same about her leg. So both parents had begun the journey in a grumpy mood.

They were barely out of town when it happened. Wendy remembered hearing her mother complain about losing a glove and her father's grunt as he bent down to pick it up, then the shock of the impact and his unaccustomed swearing as he jammed on the brake—too late!

He had jumped straight out, anxious to see what he had done to his car, and Wendy had followed. Surprisingly though, apart from the shattered windshield, the solid Old Liz was hardly damaged.

Then Edie, who had not moved, said quietly, "You'd better look at me!"

They had looked—and had a dreadful shock. She had small cuts all over her face and several deep slashes on her temple.

1. Write the topic sentence for the last paragraph. _____

2. Number these incidents in order from least important to most important (1, 2, 3, and 4).

   [ ] Wendy's mother loses a glove.   [ ] The windshield is shattered.

   [ ] Wendy's parents have a disagreement.   [ ] Edie's face is cut.

3. Who did Wendy blame for the accident? _____

4. The word "poulticing" has a meaning relating to:

   [ ] a dressing   [ ] an infection   [ ] an operation

5. Which would you consider the best title for this excerpt?

   [ ] Shattered Windshield   [ ] The Daydreamer

   [ ] The Accident   [ ] Face Wounds

6. Wendy's parents were silent because they had disagreed.   [ ] True [ ] False

7. Marjorie had been hurt in a motorbike accident.   [ ] True [ ] False

8. The family was going to town because of Edie's accident. [ ] True [ ] False

9. Who do you think is the main character in the excerpt? _____ What are your reasons?

_____

Name: _____   Date: _____

BUSH MEDICINE
by Konai Helu-Thaman

when i was a little girl   and somewhat apprehensive
many women used to come   now the wise men say
to my grandmother to be cured   that there might be something
she chewed some leaves   in my grandmother's cure
wrapped in more leaves   and the leaves that flavored it
then used the juice to dry out   i only hope that one day
the **bothersome** sores   they too would be sure
the women were always quiet

1. In this poem, it is most likely that the poet's intention is to

   (A) teach people how to prepare bush medicines.

   (B) ridicule doctors who won't accept bush medicines.

   (C) get readers to reconsider their attitude to bush medicines.

   (D) provide information on the collection of bush medicine ingredients.

2. The writer's grandmother chewed leaves

   (A) to release the juices.   (C) because she was hungry.

   (B) to help her concentrate.   (D) because she liked the taste.

3. In this poem, the word "bothersome" is closest in meaning to

   (A) painful.   (C) contagious.

   (B) annoying.   (D) unpleasant.

4. The leaves were used for

   (A) cooking food.   (C) wrapping up parcels.

   (B) making baskets.   (D) healing skin problems.

5. The wise men referred to are probably

   (A) judges.

   (B) doctors.

   (C) lawyers.

   (D) teachers.

6. The women who came to the grandmother were

   (A) wise and bothersome.

   (B) apprehensive and wise.

   (C) quiet and apprehensive.

   (D) apprehensive and bothersome.

7. In your opinion, what is the poet's attitude towards her grandmother? _____

   _____

8. What theme is developed in the poem? _____

   _____

THAT'S A JOB FOR ME!

by Ross Pearce

"Snakes are poisonous! Quick! Kill the snake!"

Many unfortunate non-venomous snakes have been killed because we do not question the truth of our preconceived notions or stereotypes. Stereotypes are fixed ideas or feelings we have about things in our world. They influence much of our thinking. Our actions are often based on the stereotypes we hold in our minds.

In the world of work, it is easy to be influenced by these fixed concepts and stereotypes. "I can't do that job; only boys do that sort of work." "I'd like to do that when I leave school but I think that's a job for women." Such ideas can greatly reduce the jobs we might think suitable for ourselves. They become like invisible chains restricting our freedom to choose from the widest range of jobs. You must wonder why people would allow themselves to be robbed of their freedom to choose.

Stereotypes sneak into our minds without our realizing it and then become part of our way of thinking.

* "Jenny loves bandaging cuts and bruises. She's going to be a nurse when she grows up."

* "Jason loves bandaging cuts and bruises. He's going to be a doctor when he grows up."

When Jenny and Jason watch television, they see that the nurses are usually women and the doctors are usually men. So little Jenny and Jason store in their minds the stereotype that girls become nurses and boys become doctors. They do not remember where the idea came from. They believe that it was what they chose freely for themselves and what they always wanted.

To understand how stereotypes sneak into our thoughts, we need to be alert for clues in what people say to us and what we hear, watch, and read in the media. Television can be very influential in developing these stereotypes in people's minds.

Luckily things are changing!

---

1. How many paragraphs are in this extract? _____

2. In the paragraph commencing "In the world of work . . . ," what is the main idea? _____

_____

3. The two sentences commencing with the asterisk (*) are very similar. The differences

are meant to show how much we are influenced by _____.

4. Which of the following statements is an example of stereotyping?

   (A)   Cathy Freeman is one of Australia's great sprinters.

   (B)   Men's sports are more exciting to watch than women's sports.

   (C)   It is important to offer your seat to an elderly person on a bus.

   (D)   Many people believe farmers should have guns to shoot feral animals.

5. How does the writer feel about stereotyping in today's society? _____

_____

6. If you had to give the extract another title, a good one would be:

   ☐ Finding a Job   ☐ Doctors and Nurses

   ☐ Reasons to Kill Snakes   ☐ Changing Attitudes

7. The theme for this passage could be: Stereotyping benefits _____ .

8. According to the text, most people probably have some fixed ideas.   ☐ True   ☐ False

9. Give an example of stereotyping you have come across. _____

_____

Name: _____   Date: _____

PERFECT TIMING
by Jeremy Fisher

Read this passage from *Perfect Timing* by Jeremy Fisher and answer the questions.

Inside the hall, streamers and balloons were in profusion. Andrew recognized the streamers and decorations he had made among the many hanging from the ceiling and walls. He was pleased that the junk material they had gathered up and recycled had turned out looking so sharp.

Gaggles of kids stood about, talking excitedly about their clothes, their hair—for some of the boys had gone for a greased-back look, and several of the girls had teased their hair into towering beehives—and, of course, the band. At the end of the hall, on a small raised platform, stood a familiar drum kit. Guitars rested on their metal stands in front of it, and a keyboard system was arranged to one side. Large speakers had been placed on either side of the platform.

Nick and Tim ran up to Andrew and Amanda.

"Andrew," Nick said excitedly, "it's fantastic! They're really here. Even after winning the awards. They've still come to play for us!"

Right then, the lights dimmed. A hush fell over the hall, and all eyes fixed on the stage.

Suddenly lights flashed and— zap!— there was the band! They began their first song to the accompaniment of great multi-colored bursts of light which swirled about them.

Once they had finished, they began another of their hits, and then another. Andrew stood transfixed as the music rolled around him. It was as if he was suspended in space somewhere, seeing and hearing everything, but invisible to all about him.

Then the band finished their **set**. The applause went on and on. Nick and Matt were whistling and stamping their feet, and shouting out their approval. Andrew, out of his spell, had yelled himself hoarse. Amanda's hands were stinging from the number of times she'd clapped them together.

1. The passage is mainly about _____.

2. What word do you think could best replace "gaggles"?

    a. groups   b. hundreds   c. an assembly   d. a collection

3. If you had to give the passage a new title, it would be:

  ☐ Space Age Music   ☐ Another Night Out   ☐ A Stunning Act   ☐ The Decorated Hall

4. Check the box to show which sentence contains the main idea for the seventh paragraph.

  ☐ Once they had finished, they began another of their hits, and then another.

  ☐ Andrew stood transfixed as the music rolled around him.

  ☐ It was as if he was suspended in space somewhere, seeing and hearing everything, but invisible to all about him.

5. When the audience arrived, the band was already on the platform. ☐ True ☐ False

6. Amanda enjoyed the show as much as Nick. ☐ True ☐ False

7. What is the "set" that is referred to in the last paragraph? _____

8. The band received (an enthusiastic   an exhausting a conventional) response. (Circle one answer.)

9. Give two ways appreciation was shown for the band. _____ _____

INTRODUCTION

Name: _____   Date: _____

Making an inference is a thinking or reasoning skill. (See also Drawing Conclusions, page 33.) The reader is often only given a limited amount of information and makes inferences from the information given. Readers also use their general knowledge when making inferences.

Read the following short passage.

Bradley walked into the room and kicked the sleeping bag to the other side of the room. The dog, sprawled on its belly, looked up for a moment then put its head back onto its outstretched front paws.	Bradley sniffed noisily and dropped his backpack onto the bare boards as he headed to the ancient fridge.

The reader could make several inferences from this passage. What sort of a person was Bradley? Why did he kick the sleeping bag? Why was the dog so disinterested? From the evidence, the reader could probably infer that Bradley was in a bad mood. Because the dog didn't react the reader might also infer that Bradley was often in a bad mood. It is likely that the room is not Bradley's usual room and that he is probably camping there. The reader might also make some inferences about how Bradley feels about his present situation.

Sometimes writers will deliberately mislead the reader. They do not give all the information or they add information that gives the reader the wrong ideas or impressions. This happens in mystery stories and some horror books.

Now read this excerpt from *Streetscape* by Ian Steep.

Michael and Nicole cautiously made their way along a side lane until they were out of sight of the street and the neighboring windows. The side fence was well protected by shrubs and vines, making it easy to get over unseen. Michael swung onto the lower branches of a big jacaranda and looked around. The leaves still covered him. Nicole perched on a branch behind him.

"Go on, get moving," she hissed.

Stealthily they crept along the branch until, stretching out, they reached the balcony. There was no movement in the house and the street was quiet. Keeping low, they picked their way between the terracotta pots and geraniums behind the balcony wall. Sliding glass doors led into the upstairs rooms. The curtains were drawn making it impossible to see inside. A thin strip of silver ran around the perimeter of the doors.

"Blast!" whispered Nicole angrily. "It's alarmed."

At the last set of doors, nearest the back of the house, there were no curtains, just a long venetian blind. The slats stood open. Michael and Nicole approached it cautiously. A gentle tug on the lock showed that the door was locked.

1. The reader could infer that Michael and Nicole are involved in a criminal act. Give one reason for this inference. _____

2. The reader can infer that Michael and Nicole may be used to this sort of activity. What evidence suggests this? _____

3. How does the author create a feeling of suspense? _____

4. The house is probably empty. This can be best inferred from the fact that

   ☐ some curtains were closed.   ☐ the balcony was scaled.   ☐ the alarm was set.

5. If something is being done "stealthily," it is done in what manner? _____ .

6. It is most likely that this is not the first time Michael and Nicole have seen the house. What reason could you give for this inference?

_____

Name: _____   Date: _____

THE LADY IN BLACK

Winter.

One in the morning, Monday June 9.

Night has leeched life from the suburbs on the surrounding hills and from the wharves around the Backwater Bay. The bus is a vulnerable glow-worm of light crawling along the wet, black road.

Brett stares absentmindedly through the window glare into the damp gloom. All he can see is the pool of yellow light racing along the road as if accompanying the bus on its **silent mission**. The road could well be part of the black surface of still water of the nearby bay. The scattered lights of the city center are lost in the cold mist that drifts across the water and seeps into the surrounding locked suburbs.

The bus stops for some T-intersection lights that carry on their relentless cycle of amber, red, green though the bus is the only traffic at this hour. It could be a ghost town. Brett stares out into the bushes growing along the roadside. A sign states that the landscaping is a government project to green the environment with natural vegetation.

Behind the saplings and bushes are the vague skeletal structures of a silent railway goods yard. Brett shivers and thinks how great it will be to get into bed. Selling hamburgers on the late night shift was not a great challenge but it gave him some holiday cash.

The bus shudders gently forward as the lights change to green.

Out of the corner of his eye Brett catches sight of a movement in a gap in the shrubbery. For a moment he thinks it his reflection in the lightly misted glass. He hadn't seen the person until she had moved and he almost called out to the driver to stop, then suddenly realized that she probably didn't want to catch the bus. It wasn't a regular bus stop.

1. The writer creates a special mood (or atmosphere) in this excerpt. In your opinion, the passage best creates a mood of

   (A) fear.   (B) sorrow.   (C) anxiety.   (D) foreboding.

2. From the information in the excerpt, Brett could best be described as . . . (Check one or more boxes.)

   ☐ aggressive.   ☐ belligerent.

   ☐ somber.   ☐ detached.

   ☐ industrious.   ☐ annoyed.

   ☐ meddlesome.   ☐ impertinent.

3. Give two words of opposite meaning that would describe the world outside the bus and the environment

   in the bus. a. _____ b. _____

4. In your opinion, what is the most important thing that happens in the passage? _____

   _____

5. Find two references (allusions) to death in the excerpt.

   a. _____ b. _____

6. The bus has a "silent mission." What do you think that mission might be? _____

   _____

7. Which word best describe Brett's attitude towards his job?   ☐ indifference   ☐ dedication

Name: _____   Date: _____

ODIOUS UNDERARMUS, MARATHON MAN
by Bill Condon and Dianne Bates

CHARACTERS—<u>Odious Underarmus</u>: fishmonger, <u>Billious</u>: Odious's friend, <u>Jilly Achilles</u>: a maiden, <u>Regurgitus</u>: Jilly's handmaiden, <u>Achilles</u>: Jilly's father, <u>Tyrannus Dreadus</u>: Jilly's betrothed, <u>Narratus</u>: the Oracle, and a crowd

SCENE 1: A crowded market place in ancient Greece.

ODIOUS: *(calling)* Salmon, snapper, sardines, stingray, shark, squid, shrimp, swordfish, sole, sturgeon, seal! Freshly caught last week! Getcha red-hot fishies. Salmon, snapper . . .

(He continues to mime as Narratus steps forward from the crowd.)

NARRATUS: Ladies and gentlemen, welcome to a typical day in the tiny Grecian village of Athos in the year 776 B.C. Behind me is a typical smelly fishmonger of these parts, Odious Underarmus, selling typically smelly fish. What Odious does not realize is that any minute now, the course of his life is going to dramatically change—in fact, what you are about to witness is the beginning of a "whimsical" romance.

(Jilly, Achilles, and Regurgitus enter.)

REGURGITUS: Hurry along now, Jilly. You know we'll be in trouble if they find out we're from Sparta.

JILLY: Don't be so cowardly, Regurgitus. A Spartan has no fear of anything, let alone these imbecilic Athenians.

ODIOUS: Salmon, snapper, sea lion, stingray. Getcha red-hot fishies. Fish, miss? Care for some week-old fishies?

JILLY: Do you have any smoked shicklebocks?

ODIOUS: I smoked the last one yesterday.

JILLY: Well, do you have any nice eyes? *(Pause)* Why did I say nice eyes?

ODIOUS: Because you have—you have nice eyes.

REGURGITUS: Oh, oh! I've seen that look before.

NARRATUS: The look of love!

REGURGITUS: Exactly! I don't like the look of this. Hurry, Jilly! Let's go.

JILLY: *(to Odious)* I do like your looks, Mr. . . . Mr. . . . ?

ODIOUS: Odious Underarmus, Miss.

REGURGITUS: This can't go any further, Jilly. Your father would never agree to you having anything to do with an Athenian.

JILLY: An oracle once told me I would **hook** the man of my dreams . . .

ODIOUS: My mom always said I was a **good catch**.

1. The intended audience for a production of this play would most likely be _____ .

2. A number of the characters' names are

   (A) names from ancient Greece.   (C) meant to give authenticity and dignity to the play.

   (B) common, modern Grecian names.   (D) names referring to unpleasant human functions.

3. This play could best be described as

   (A) a comedy.   (B) a tragedy.   (C) educational.

4. What is the importance of the words "hook" and "good catch"? _____

_____

5. Make two observations about the fish Odious is selling.

   a. _____   b. _____

6. From the information in the play, you would infer that Odious is

   (A) an official.   (B) a buffoon.   (C) an idealist.   (D) a leader.

7. A person who is "betrothed" is (married, promised, disobedient, impaired). (Circle one answer.)

Name: _____   Date: _____

POLITICALLY CORRECT
by Greg Anderson-Clift

Read this short comic strip in which Max (tall) and Leon (short) visit a pet shop.

1. Humor in comics often depends upon "misunderstandings." In your opinion, who in this comic

   strip most misunderstands the situation? _____

2. In your opinion, are any of the comic characters stereotyped? (Yes / No)

   If "Yes," who? _____ How? _____

3. Comics often make use of facial features. What inferences can you make about the expression of the

   pet shop owner in frame 3? _____

4. Comic characters often overreact or underreact. Which character, in your opinion, would be

   least stressed by the situation shown in the last frame? _____

5. How would pet lovers react to the last frame?

   (A) amused but upset   (B) angry and appalled

   (C) depressed and helpless   (D) pleased but weary

6. Comics often comment on social issues. What issue do you think is being commented upon in this

   comic strip? _____

AN INTERVIEW WITH PAUL MURPHY

from Radio Current Affairs by Elizabeth Halley

MAKING INFERENCES

This is the beginning of an interview with Paul Murphy, an Australian radio current affairs broadcaster. The interviewer is Elizabeth Halley. Interviews are recorded in a similar way to the dialogue of a play.

Elizabeth Halley: What do you do on radio?

Paul Murphy: I am a broadcaster of a current affairs program called "PM." PM provides an analysis of what is happening in Australia and the rest of the world.

EH: What do you do as a broadcaster of current affairs?

PM: You give introductions to reports and conduct comments on interviews. I imagine that 35 percent and sometimes 70 percent of the program is me doing interviews. You're a broadcaster that is reliable. Your audience might only listen to you once or twice a week but they know you are there.

EH: Can somebody else stand in for you if you are sick?

PM: I make a point of never being sick! I've always been there and that's the way you can build up an audience. I was a Canberra correspondent in 1969. I can call people like the Secretary of the Treasury personally and ask a favor, because I've been around as long as he has. In this way the program can include famous or sought-after personalities.

EH: So there are important people you know and can contact, and that makes you very valuable to PM?

PM: I think that's how the employers see it. It's just familiarity—I've been a part of journalism both here and overseas, and in television, so a lot of people know me.

EH: What sort of contact do you have with your audience—do they call up?

PM: People don't often take the step of calling, but when they do I take every call.

EH: What sort of things do people say when they write in?

PM: People contact us for a variety of reasons. Perhaps two percent of every communication you get is thanking you for something. Mainly, it's annoyance, saying, "You should know more about the story, are you aware that . . . ?" It's all part of the information gathering process. Often you feel you want to cut yourself off, but that's death professionally. You can't—you have got to know what people think and feel, even if you profoundly disagree with them.

1. From the interview, Paul Murphy could best be described as

(A) a committed broadcaster.   (C) an intolerant broadcaster.

(B) an opinionated broadcaster.   (D) a nonchalant broadcaster.

2. As an interviewer, Elizabeth Halley could best be described as

☐ sympathetic.   ☐ aggressive.   ☐ forthright.   ☐ persistent.

3. What does Paul Murphy mean when he says, ". . . that's death professionally"?

_____

4. The relationship between the interviewer and interviewee could best be described as

☐ cautious.   ☐ tense.   ☐ cordial.   ☐ informal.

5. Paul Murphy's journalistic experience makes him a valued broadcaster.   ☐ True   ☐ False

6. It is likely that most people who listen to PM _____ Paul Murphy's presentation.

(verb)

Name: _____   Date: _____

BOOK REVIEW

Code of Deception **by Ted Ottley**

This is a story of revenge. It is an electronics-based, science fiction, adventure thriller. There are obvious goodies and baddies and a range of characters whose sympathies and intentions are slowly revealed. It is a story of Lear Jets, mysterious cars, bugging, drugs, and corruption in high places.

Jake Carson, at fifteen, is a swimming coach and computer genius. He lives happily with his father. Unknown to him, his life is under threat from the neo-Nazi Dr. Mulder. Because Jake's grandfather allegedly stole the plans for the **prototype** of an electronic game from the doctor, Jake and his father become the focus of the doctor's **unrelenting revenge obsession**. Mulder has destroyed the family company and is bent on destroying the Carson family. He uses his twisted brilliance to develop a virtual reality computer game that can also simulate emotions—virtual emotions—which were obtained through the use of real encounters with death.

Ted Ottley's journalistic style is fast moving with sudden breaks and moves. The story is compact and of the moment, even though it weaves a web of intrigue across three generations. There are no loose ends. The climax is frightening and the epilogue is sinister and is an obvious opening for a sequel.

The story raises obvious moral questions, not only about the ethics of company espionage, but just where the ever increasing pace of technological change is leading the world. Do we still have control over our own lives?

from *Magpies Magazine*

1. From the points made in the review, a reader could infer that the reviewer

    (A) was receptive to the book's style.

    (B) found the book lacked credibility.

    (C) found little to recommend the book.

    (D) was critical of the book's subject matter.

2. The review was most likely written for the benefit of . . . (Check one box.)

    ☐ the author.   ☐ the publisher.   ☐ journalists.   ☐ librarians.

3. A "prototype" is

    (A) the group of failed models.

    (B) a standard production model.

    (C) one of the first models tested.

    (D) one in a series of commercial models.

4. Why does the character, Dr. Mulder, want to take revenge on Jake and his father?

    _____

5. Referring to the text, what word would you use to describe Dr. Mulder? _____

6. A person who has an "unrelenting revenge obsession" could be described as

    (consumed by hate   paralyzed by delusion   goaded by fear). (Circle one answer.)

7. Would the book appeal to you? _____ Why? _____

8. Use the numbers 1, 2, and 3 to sequence the order in which events happened (from first to last).

    ☐ Carson's family company is destroyed.

    ☐ The plans for an electronic game are allegedly stolen.

    ☐ At fifteen, Jake is a computer genius and swimming coach.

9. How are virtual emotions obtained? _____

28

Name: _____   Date: _____

INTRODUCTION

Sometimes, when we read, we are not always directly told all the information. Often we can work out what is happening, how people feel, or where the action is by information in the writing. The context can also give clues to the meaning of new or unusual words.

Read this short passage from *Circles* by William Taylor.

> Today I pushed my way through the undergrowth, doing my best to follow the ill-formed track to the spot beneath the giant rimu tree where a slab of marble says: Elizabeth Costello 1840–1876 and John Costello 1839–1876. My father, foolish man, lost spirit, survived his wife by no more than a handful of hours. Robert and I dug his grave and then we left this place with, in reality, little hope of ever seeing it again.

From the text, we get clues about what might be going on: something sorrowful seems to be taking place (the narrator is visiting his parents' graves in some neglected place). There is also a sense of loneliness (the narrator is alone in an isolated environment). We get this information from the context in which it appears. We use **context clues**.

Read this extract from *The Incredible Experience of Megan Kingsley* by Pamela O'Connor.

> A loud scraping noise sent her to the window again. The loose sheet of corrugated iron was being blown across the ground. Rain had not yet begun to fall, but the clouds were so low and menacing that Megan shivered as she sat and watched them. What a horrible, swirling black nightmare was out there!
>
> She backed away from the window. The strange stabbing feeling in her stomach became worse and she lay down on her bed, knees drawn up under her chin, wondering what terrible disaster was going to overtake them. She tried to tell herself she was being foolish, but the feeling would not go away.
>
> Megan felt a tugging at her arm and Annabel climbed in next to her. "I don't like the storm, Megan. I'm frightened."
>
> Megan hugged her.
>
> "Is the island going to blow away?"
>
> "No, of course not."
>
> "Are you sure the teddy will still be all right?"
>
> "I'm sure." A small lie wouldn't hurt.
>
> "D'you think Aurora's frightened of storms?"
>
> "She probably is. She's the same as you and me."
>
> "No, she isn't." Annabel's voice was muffled against Megan's shoulder. "She's special."
>
> Megan said nothing. What was there to say?
>
> When Mrs. Kingsley came in later to see why everyone was so quiet, she found them all in Megan's bed. All sound asleep—Annabel in Megan's arms and Patrick curled up like a puppy at the end of the bed.

1. The storm that Megan sees out the window

   (A) is pelting the house.   (B) is approaching.   (C) has passed.   (D) is spent.

2. Why do you think Megan told a lie to Annabel? _____

_____

3. Why was Annabel's voice muffled? _____

4. What do you think caused the pain in Megan's stomach? _____

5. Megan could best be described as being selfish. ☐ True ☐ False

6. About how old do you think Annabel is? _____ Why? (briefly) _____

7. What reason can you suggest for Megan NOT replying to Annabel? _____

_____

Name: _____   Date: _____

THE SECOND PLANE

Aaron looked out the small window. Great sun-drenched islands of rounded clouds stretched to the horizon. The scene hadn't changed much in the last thirty minutes.

Through breaks in the clouds he caught fleeting glimpses of the azure ocean below.

Aaron was about to look back to his book when he caught sight of another plane disappearing behind a small bank of billowing clouds. He hadn't really expected to see another plane in this part of the world. A fleeting moment of uneasiness shadowed his travel-weary mind.

When the plane emerged from behind the clouds, he guessed it was quite large even though it was still a long way off. It was certainly much larger than the inter-island Bandierante he was on.

There was a brief moment of turbulence. Unconsciously, Aaron tapped the inhaler he carried in his denim jacket.

The new plane was turning, starting to descend in a huge arc.

A vague sense of apprehension furrowed Aaron's brow.

Aaron touched his mother's elbow. She looked up and smiled as he pointed through the round window. His mother leaned across and peered out across the clouds.

After a moment she looked at him inquiringly. "What was it?" She spoke slowly, mouthing the words over the roar of the twin engines.

Aaron took a quick look but the plane had disappeared. He shrugged his shoulders and forced a smile.

His mother copied his actions and returned to her leaflet of Autitaki's tourist attractions.

Aaron looked out the window. The lonely sky seemed to go on forever. The deserted ocean appeared endless. He resisted the urge to tap his inhaler and returned to his book his father had insisted he take on vacations. But he was **reading the words and not connecting with the story**.

Absentmindedly he looked out the window. To his amazement the other plane was just emerging from a mass of misty cloud. For a brief, heart-stopping moment he thought the planes might collide. He quickly realized that it was passing right under the little Air Rarotonga Bandierante. Its details were clear.

---

1. Name two actions that suggest Aaron was troubled.

a) _____   b) _____

2. Aaron arrived at the Cook Islands on a

☐ 747 jet   ☐ Bandierante   ☐ four engine, propeller-driven plane

3. Give one word to describe how Aaron's mother was feeling during the trip. _____

4. Explain your choice. _____

5. Aaron's mother was preoccupied with (Circle one word.)

(air safety   vacation plans   Aaron's medication   weather conditions).

6. The phrase, "reading the words but not connecting with the story," suggests that Aaron

☐ couldn't understand the story.   ☐ found the words too difficult to read.

☐ kept losing his place on the page.   ☐ was reading without thinking about the meaning.

7. Aaron tapped his inhaler out of habit.   ☐ True   ☐ False

8. Aaron's father had insisted that Aaron take a book during his vacation.   ☐ True   ☐ False

9. This is the start of a story. The writing style indicates it will most likely be a(n) _____ story.

Name: _____   Date: _____

SPECIAL DAY

There was one special day I remember,
  when the sun set fire to the sky,
and I was at the blue-rimmed beach,
and I ran skidding down the steep green hill
  to the silver-glinting shore.
The white-topped waves swung skywards
  recklessly,
maybe trying to put out the fire in the sky.
I thrust myself at the ocean,
  snatching for action
not wanting to waste one greedy moment,
not wanting to miss one searching wave.
It was a good day, that special day,
it had a good beginning
  and no real ending:
there were no clocks out there
  where the waves **wallowed** on the sand:

no radios screamed out the seconds
  and the minutes
  and the hours . . .
Eventually, I suppose, the day ended,
and the night must have swallowed up the fire,
and I must have plodded up the green hill
sometime.
Days have passed since then,
Days without number.
Days and nights; time;
oceans of time.
Yet that one day, that special day,
clings on to me forever,
with the sun setting fire to the sky
  and the sand on the shore glinting silver
  and the white topped waves reaching out for
me . . .

by David Bateson (1977)

---

1. The special day was a day spent

  (A) surfing.   (B) climbing hills.   (C) writing poetry. (D) listening to the radio.

2. This poem was most likely written

  (A) during the time on the beach.   (C) when the poet had returned home.

  (B) before skidding down the green hill.   (D) a long time after the actual event.

3. For the poet, the special day could be best described as

  (A) memorable.   (B) traditional.   (C) typical.   (D) ordinary.

4. The lines:
    no radios screamed out the seconds
    and the minutes
    and the hours . . .

  are most likely intended to show how

  (A) lonesome the poet was.   (C) much fun the poet was having.

  (B) time did not matter to the poet.   (D) the poet kept a check on time.

5. The poem creates a feeling of

  (A) regret.   (B) sorrow.   (C) hope.   (D) nostalgia.

6. The word "wallowed" means to

  (A) roll about.   (B) crash down.   (C) sweep over.   (D) tumble into.

7. How did the poet feel after his special day?

  (A) contented   (B) melancholy   (C) depressed   (D) excited

8. In your opinion, how old was the poet on the special day? about _____

9. What information in the poem supports your conclusion? _____

USING CONTEXT CLUES

RUGBY UNION

from *Sport in the Making* by Shane Power

The game of Rugby began in the middle of a traditional English soccer game in 1823. William Webb Ellis was a student at the famous Rugby School in England. He was playing in an interclass match when he suddenly felt like picking the ball up. He did just that and raced off to the other end of the field with the ball tucked under his arm. Players and spectators were astonished. This action was against the rules and caused Ellis's team to look foolish. It did not take long for the news of the incident to spread to other schools. Football enthusiasts were talking about it and arguing for and against the handling of the ball.

Some players liked the idea of running with the ball so much that they introduced this new rule into the game. The students at Cambridge University were among those who were "having a go at the game of Rugby." At first, a player could only run with the ball if it was a fair catch. It took many years for this game to be accepted by schools and clubs. Rugby College itself did not play the new rule until 18 years after the Ellis incident.

By 1848, so many schools had introduced the rule that a meeting was called to draw up a common list of rules for everyone to follow. At this stage, the game was only played in schools and universities. It was called Rugby, or Rugger, after the school where Ellis performed his feat.

By 1872, 21 clubs had formed an amateur organization which they called Rugby Union. No professional football players were allowed to play the game. Each team fielded 20 players but this was later reduced to 15 a side, the same as today's teams.

The first international Rugby match was played between England and Scotland in the same year that Rugby Union was formed. The Scottish team won that historic match. It was only a matter of time before the game had spread far and wide to other parts of the world, including France, the United States, New Zealand, and Africa.

1. Richard Ellis's action could best be described as . . . (Check one box.)

☐ predictable. ☐ preventable. ☐ impetuous. ☐ hazardous.

2. In your opinion, why did it take Rugby many years to catch on? _____

_____

3. Why was the first international Rugby match played against Scotland?

(A) The Scottish people didn't play soccer.
(B) Scotland is just across a land border from England.
(C) The Scots had been playing Rugby longer than the English.
(D) There were no professional football players in Scotland.

4. Why was the new game called "Rugby"? Give your reason. _____

_____

5. Number the boxes (1, 2, 3, and 4) to show the sequence in which events happened.

☐ The students at Cambridge begin playing Rugby.

☐ Ellis disrupts a soccer match by picking up the ball.

☐ An organization called Rugby Union is formed.

☐ The new game was called Rugby after the school where Ellis first performed his feat.

6. It was a while before Rugby was played outside school situations. ☐ True ☐ False

Name: _____   Date: _____

INTRODUCTION

Drawing conclusions is an advanced reading skill. It requires you to make a judgment about what you have read. It may involve finding the main idea (page 17), making inferences (page 23), and using context clues (page 29). It is related to other reading skills, such as recognizing fact and opinion (page 50) and being able to distinguish between relevant and irrelevant information (page 53).

A conclusion is reached by reasoning (thinking about a situation). You may be required to have an opinion or make a decision. You may have to justify your opinion or reason. Drawing conclusions can only be done after you have read the whole excerpt (or story) —when you have all the information.

Read the article "Warbirds over Wanaka" by Shiri Gounder, and answer the questions.

Wanaka is a scenic little town about 80 km north-west of Queenstown in New Zealand. It stays fairly dry and sunny, and despite the snow-capped peaks in the distance, temperatures remain mild. Wanaka is popular with tourists and seems to have a disproportionate number of hotels and motels.

Every two years, though, over the long Easter weekend, Wanaka's normal influx of visitors positively explodes—75,000 people drawn by a three-day air show called "Warbirds over Wanaka."

Aviation buffs make up most of the crowd, but the display of ex-military vehicles, vintage motorcycles, farm machinery, and antique fire engines has a certain appeal, as well.

On the ground the vintage aircraft look spectacular. In the air, they're even more awesome, with aerial flying and stunt displays performed by the RNZAF Red Checkers and the Roaring Forties Harvard aerobatic teams.

In the 1998 Easter show, the warbirds had a predominantly Russian theme—five Polikarpov 1-16s of the Alpine Fighter Collection (the only ones flying in the world); a Russian Sukhoi Su-31, flown by Australian aerobatic champion Nigel Arnot; and a MiG-15, which flew a mock dogfight against a similar vintage P51 Mustang. Even a Catalina flying boat, a PBY which should be familiar to Kiwis, had a red star on its tail.

It was a rich assortment of aircraft, military and otherwise: stunt planes like the Boeing Stearman and Tiger Moth; training planes like the Harvards; warbirds like Corsairs, Spitfires and Mustangs . . . the planes that made history and, in some cases, turned the tide of world events.

And there is still time to reserve one of those Wanaka motels for the next big show.

1. The writer finds the air show at Wanaka

   (A) provincial.   (B) excessive.   (C) wondrous.   (D) predictable.

2. What information leads you to the conclusion that the organizer of the air show did a good job?

   _____

3. Most of the time, Wanaka could be described as (peaceful   distinguished   exciting). (Circle one answer.)

4. A good title for the excerpt would be ☐ Wanaka Warplanes   ☐ Hotels of Wanaka

5. What information leads you to the conclusion that the show is not just for air enthusiasts?

   _____

6. Most of the year, there is little to attract tourists to Wanaka.   ☐ True   ☐ False

7. The people of Wanaka would find that the article paints

   (an idealistic   a sentimental   a positive   a dubious) picture of their town. (Circle one answer.)

Name: _____   Date: _____

PUDDING RECIPES

from Roland Harvey's *Book of Christmas* by Roland Harvey

The exercises on this page are based upon recipes for Australian puddings. (*Note:* A billy can is an Australian name for a utensil used to boil water, make tea, and cook any liquid on a campfire.)

Billy Can Pudding
- 1½ cups raisins
- 1 cup sugar
- ½ teaspoon mixed spice and cinnamon
- 2 cups plain flour
- 1 teaspoon baking soda
- 500 mL boiling tea

Combine all ingredients. Mix well with 500 mL of boiling tea. Empty into greased and floured billy can. Cover. Stand overnight. Steam 3½ hours.

The Cattleman's Plum Pudding
- 250 g rice
- sweetened water
- sugar
- 125 g raisins
- handful of nuts

Put rice in saucepan or billy can with boiling, sweetened water and simmer until no water is left. Add remaining ingredients. Sweeten to taste.

---

1. These recipes are most likely meant for a

   (A) family on a camping vacation.   (B) chef in a restaurant.

   (C) meal at home.   (D) birthday party.

2. What conclusions do you draw about the origins of these recipes? _____

_____

3. Which of these statements is true?

   (A) Both puddings must be cooked in an oven.

   (B) The Billy Can Pudding is mixed with water.

   (C) It takes 3½ hours to make the Cattleman's Plum Pudding.

   (D) The Billy Can Pudding needs raisins, mixed spice, and cinnamon.

4. A "floured" billy can would

   (A) be rolled in flour.   (C) be dusted inside with flour.

   (B) have roses painted on it.   (D) have a brand of flour stamped on it.

5. To make the Cattleman's Plum Pudding, you would need

   (A) rice, sugar, raisins, and nuts.

   (B) raisins, spice, cinnamon, and nuts.

   (C) cinnamon, rice, raisins, and currants.

   (D) rice, mixed spice, and raisins.

billy can

6. What features do most of the ingredients in these recipes have in common?

_____

_____

7. After studying these recipes, a reader would conclude they came from a book about

   (A) caring for sheep.   (B) cooking for a family.

   (C) the Australian outback.   (D) growing your own food.

8. What word would you use to describe the cost of preparing these puddings? _____

9. Which pudding takes longer to prepare? _____

TSUNAMI

A **tsunami** (soo-nah-mee/noun) is a series of long, high sea waves caused by a disturbance of ocean floor or seismic movement. [Jap.–tsu: harbor, nami: wave]

A tsunami is not a tidal wave. It has nothing to do with tides. They can be caused by earthquakes, volcanic action on the ocean floor, volcanoes dumping huge amounts of material into the ocean, and coastal and marine landslides. Large meteors plunging into the ocean may also cause tsunamis.

1883: Java and Sumatra

The largest tsunami in historical times was generated by the eruption of the Krakatoa volcano in 1883. The island that was Krakatoa was literally blown apart. The tsunami generated impacted the nearby islands of Java and Sumatra, with waves as high as 40 m. Approximately 36,000 people were drowned.

1946: Hawaii and California

In 1946 a magnitude 7.2 on the Richter Scale submarine earthquake occurred near Unimak Island, Alaska, and it was about five hours later that tsunamis hit the Hawaiian Islands. The wave, less than one meter in height in the open ocean, raced across the Pacific Ocean at speeds of about

800 km/hr and as it encountered the shallow waters in Hilo Harbor, over 5,000 kilometers away, it rose to a breaking wave of some 18 meters high. It demolished 500 homes and killed 159 people. It also reached the California coast where it killed several people.

Today, the Tsunami Warning System in Hawaii keeps a round-the-clock **vigil** using computers and satellites. If a tsunami is confirmed, warnings are transmitted to all potentially threatened points in the Pacific.

1998: Papua New Guinea

The recent tsunami in Papua New Guinea resulted from a shallow underwater earthquake, 30 kilometers off the north coast, generating a succession of three waves rising to heights of 10 meters. Three villages, Arop, Nimas, and Waropu, were completely destroyed while others received extensive damage. The three devastated villages had a population of 8,000 inhabitants and so far 6,000 have been unaccounted for. Reports indicate that it was mostly the elderly and children who were killed in the disaster.

The tsunami was totally unexpected and no warning system would have helped due to the close proximity to the earthquake center.

1. Which event is the least likely to be the cause of a tsunami?
   - (A) an earthquake
   - (B) a landslide
   - (C) a falling meteor
   - (D) a volcanic explosion

2. From the information it can be concluded tsunamis are rare events. ☐ True ☐ False

3. Tsunamis are most dangerous when they (Check two boxes.)

   ☐ reach shallow water.   ☐ have their origins close to the shore.

   ☐ turn into tidal waves.   ☐ are recorded on the Tsunami Warning System.

4. A "vigil" is a type of (keeping watch   judgment   record   protection). (Circle one answer.)

5. A warning system could have saved lives in Papua New Guinea. ☐ True ☐ False

6. The word "tsunami" is of _____ origin.

7. The 1883 tsunami was caused by a(n) _____ and the 1946 tsunami was

   caused by a(n) _____ .

8. Which of the above disasters caused the greatest loss of life? _____

9. It could be concluded that a reading of 7.2 on the Richter Scale is a (high   low) reading. (Circle one answer.)

Name: _____   Date: _____

THE TATTOOED MAN

By Howard Pease

Mel stared at the black panther across the silver bar. It was shiny and sleek and its eyes seemed to glint as it gently rolled its lithe muscles.

He could almost see the claws.

The bus pitched into the bus stop. The doors pulled open and there was a jostle as people pressed towards the exit, eager to get off but reluctant to face the damp night air.

Mel turned to the wet, exhausted street, choked with sodden traffic. It was early evening and the neons from the shops were making shimmering splashes of lurid color across the shiny, black surface of the road. Black like the coat of the panther. Shimmering like the panther's eyes.

The bus pulled back into the stream of traffic.

Mel turned back to the panther. With each movement of the man's shoulder, it seemed to come to life, gently flexing. Its torso seemed to swell and subside and it appeared to be climbing up the man's shoulder muscle as he turned the pages in the magazine he was reading.

The bus came to a sudden halt. Some fool had dashed through the slow-moving traffic. There was a red burst of tail lights. In the bus, standing passengers lurched forward, grabbing for rails and the backs of seats. Several horns blasted before the pedestrian hit the other side of the wide street—pretending to be oblivious of the trauma he had just created. Then he was lost in the damp, clammy crowd.

The tattooed man looked around trying to determine the cause for the sudden confusion.

The bus grunted forward.

Pressing the stop button, the man stood up, the jaguar almost lost under the white ragged threads of his sleeveless denim jacket. Mel watched him move towards the back exit.

---

1. Suggest an appropriate title for the excerpt. _____

2. Choose the statements that create the impression that something sinister may happen in the story.

   (A) Mel stared at the black panther across the silver bar.

   (B) The bus pulled back into the stream of traffic.

   (C) He could almost see the claws.

   (D) Then he was lost in the damp, clammy crowd.

   (E) Some fool had dashed through the slow moving traffic.

3. After reading the first few lines, what conclusions did you make about Mel's whereabouts?

   _____

4. The words and descriptions in the passage create a tense, suspenseful mood. What information helps you make this conclusion? (Check your choices.)

   ☐ the dark night   ☐ the bus passengers   ☐ the silver bar

   ☐ the tattoo   ☐ the foolish pedestrian   ☐ the panther's eyes

5. It is reasonable to conclude that Mel knew the tattooed man. ☐ True ☐ False

6. Which person is more likely to be in the story at a later stage?

   ☐ the person who ran across the road   ☐ the tattooed man

7. Highlight the words that compare the bus to a work animal.

Name: _____   Date: _____

INTRODUCTION

Details play an important part in written works. Details help to give the reader a clearer understanding of the story or the topic. Details can give different types of writing its particular "flavor" and often allow the reader to draw conclusions. (See page 33.) When looking at detail in factual material, we must determine whether or not it is appropriate to our purpose or studies. (See Relevant and Irrelevant Information, page 53.)

Read the following information from *"Old Faithful" Erupts in Space* **by Jeff Hecht.**

In the core of the galaxy Messier 101, something stirs every 11 million years. Astronomers, led by Ward Moody at Brigham Young University in Provo, Utah, say that M101 contains a space "geyser" that periodically ejects large volumes of gas.

M101 is a typical spiral galaxy about 24 million light years from Earth, which we view nearly face-on. It appears unremarkable in standard images but when the Moody group looked at M101 through a filter that blocked starlight and highlighted the emissions of interstellar clouds of hydrogen, they saw three knots of gas arranged in an "S" shape, which appeared to have been shot out from the center of the galaxy.

The details give the reader some idea of just how spectacular this space discovery was.

1. What details suggest that the event described was of gigantic proportions?

Answer: The vast distances and times involved (24 million light years, every 11 million years).

2. Give one detail that shows that most astronomers thought that M101 was commonplace.

_____

3. Who, or what, is Brigham Young? _____

Continue your reading of *"Old Faithful" Erupts in Space*.

Active galaxies also eject material from their cores, but these jets are thought to approach the speed of light. By contrast, the knots of gas in M101 seem to be moving sedately at around 100 kilometers per second. Judging from the knots' positions, the geyser's eruptions occur at intervals of about 11 million years, and in alternate directions, shooting out on opposite sides of M101's core.

The astronomers believe that the eruptions occur as black holes pass back and forth through a bar of gas near M101's center. The faster eruptions in active galaxies are also thought to be caused by black holes. The sluggishness of the knots in M101 suggest that its black hole must be much smaller than black holes in other galaxies.

"If it's not a black hole, we are in an even **tighter spot** trying to explain it," says Moody.

4. What detail tells the reader that M101 is a little different from some other galaxies?

  (A) Its distance from Earth.   (C) The speed at which its geysers eject.

  (B) The angle at which it is observed.   (D) Its eruptions are caused by black holes.

5. What makes researchers think that the black hole of M101 is smaller than black holes of active

   galaxies? _____

6. How fast is material being ejected from M101's core? _____

7. The phrase, "tighter spot," means _____.

8. How confident is Moody of his explanation? ☐ highly ☐ moderately ☐ not very

9. What shape is a typical galaxy? _____

Name: _____   Date: _____

GLOBAL WARMING

From *Technology for the Environment* by Mike Callaghan and Peter Knapp

The Earth's climate has changed over millions of years. Places that were once rainforests are now deserts; places which are now on the tops of mountains, hundreds of kilometers from the sea, were once on the ocean floor. Sometimes the climatic changes have been small and could only be noticed by sensitive scientific instruments. At other times they have been extreme.

The ice ages are an example of climatic change. Ice from the polar regions expanded, reaching areas thousands of kilometers away. During the last ice age, humans had to change their lifestyles greatly. They used technology such as fire, the ability to make clothing and shelter, and most importantly, the capacity to think and solve problems to ensure their survival. Animals that could not change or move to warmer regions died.

For millions of years climatic changes were due to natural causes rather than the activities of human beings. However, since the Industrial Revolution over 200 years ago, the actions of people and their use of machines has had a greater and greater effect on the world's climate. Perhaps the greatest influence has been the greenhouse effect.

The amount of greenhouse gases released into the atmosphere since the Industrial Revolution has increased hugely. This is because of the increased use of cars, the clearing and burning of forests, the way people use the planet for food production, and the way people live, using appliances such as air-conditioners and heaters. The greenhouse gases that are the result of human activities rise into the atmosphere and act like a blanket to decrease the amount of radiated heat.

In Australia, scientists predict that there will be a rise in the sea levels with more floods and droughts, and the snowline in the snow field of NSW and Victoria will recede. Parts of inland Australia will receive more rainfall and the cyclone belt of Northern Australia will move further south. There is also the prediction that these changes will affect Australia's energy resources, agriculture, and tourist industries. The transport we use, the way we communicate, and even our health may be affected.

---

1. Climatic change has been a feature of the climate since Earth was formed.

Draw lines from "Ancient" or "Recent" to show the features of such climatic change.

- an increase in greenhouse gases

Ancient
- generally of natural cause
- happened slowly

Recent
- rainforests turned to deserts
- icecaps expand

2. If the Earth gets warmer, there will be more deserts in Australia. ☐ True ☐ False

Using one or two words, complete these three sentences about the greenhouse effect.

3. The amount of greenhouse gases in the atmosphere is _____ .

4. The greenhouse problem began with the _____ .

5. Greenhouse gases are a result of _____ .

Find words in the passage to complete these sentences.

6. Humans had to change their _____ during the last ice age.

7. Scientists predict that there will be more _____ and _____ .

8. Humans survived the ice ages because they had the ability to _____ technology.

9. Scientists predict the Victorian snowfield will get (colder   smaller   deeper). (Circle one answer.)

Name: _____   Date: _____

MARAUDING ELEPHANTS FEEL THE HEAT

by Jonathan Beard

A pepper spray that deters elephants from raiding farms is being developed by a **zoologist** at the University of Cambridge and an inventor in the USA.

"In Asia, elephants destroy thousands of dollars worth of crops each year," says Loki Osborn, the Cambridge zoologist. The problem is also increasing in Africa, says Osborn, as elephants are attracted to this rich source of food.

On both continents, the traditional way of combating the problem is to try to frighten the animals away by shouting at them, beating drums, and throwing rocks. Elephants that raid crops are shot. "In Zimbabwe, at least a hundred elephants are killed each year during problem-animal control actions," says Osborn, "but this does little to reduce crop damage."

Osborn is working with Jack Birochak, an inventor based at Valley Forge, PA, who has developed pepper sprays to deter grizzly bears. The spray can holds about one kilogram of a mixture of chili pepper and oil.

Because of the obvious difficulties of operating a spray can close to a wild elephant, Birochak is developing a compressed air launcher that can throw the can as far as two hundred meters. The launcher is aimed at an area near the elephants; and when the can hits the ground, it begins spraying. Alternatively, it can be set to start spraying in mid-air.

Tests on wild elephants in Zimbabwe have shown that pepper spray does work. "The elephant, with its long nose lined with mucous membranes, has one of the most **acute**—and sensitive—senses of smell in the animal kingdom," Osborn says. In the tests, he says, the elephants would first freeze, then blow their noses before leaving quickly. The chili causes no permanent harm.

Osborn hopes that tests of the compressed air launcher in Cambridge will be successful. "The next step will be to test it on elephants in Zimbabwe this summer."

---

1. Draw a line to match the details that apply to each person.

   Loki Osborn is developing   a spray to deter elephants.

   Jack Birochak developed   a pepper spray to deter bears.

2. Who is developing the spray can launcher? _____

3. The compressed air spray can launcher will be first tested in

   ☐ Cambridge.   ☐ Pennsylvania.   ☐ Zimbabwe.   ☐ Asia.

4. Elephants have one of the most sensitive animal noses.   ☐ True   ☐ False

5. Shouting at elephants is used to protect crops.   ☐ True   ☐ False

6. Elephants are raiding farms to escape pepper-can attacks.   ☐ True   ☐ False

7. The elephant-deterring sprays are being developed in Africa.   ☐ True   ☐ False

8. Why do you think the pepper spray is being developed? _____

   _____

9. A zoologist is a person who studies _____.

10. Pepper spray has been successfully used on _____.

11. In the passage, the word "acute" could best be replaced with . . . (Check one box.)

   ☐ pointed.   ☐ keen.   ☐ crucial.   ☐ brisk.

FOLLOWING DIRECTIONS

INTRODUCTION

If we want to know how to do something, we have to follow a procedure or, as some people say, **follow directions** or instructions. You may have books at home that tell you how to do things. Books with many sets of directions are called manuals. Some people have manuals for making repairs. They can be called "how-to" books.

Some directions/instructions are simple. A machine at a ferry terminal has instructions on how to purchase a ticket. We call each part of the directions (instructions) steps. People follow directions nearly every day of their lives.

Directions/instructions have two basic forms:

1. Some instructions follow a sequence of steps to achieve a goal. Examples include recipes, "how to" put things together, "how to" play games, and so on. Diagrams are often used to supplement the written instructions.

2. Other instructions are not set out in sequential form. Examples include instructions on "how to" care for a car, "how to" enjoy a holiday.

Pineapple Scones ◄——————————— the aim/goal (what you will make).

Serves 4 ◄——————————— How many people you will be serving.

Ingredients ◄——————————— (often called *materials needed* in instructions other than recipes.)

- 2 cups of self-rising flour
- 30 g butter or margarine
- 1 egg
- 450 g can crushed pineapple, drained
- ½ tablespoon mixed spices

- 1 tablespoon sugar
- ½ cup water
- 1 tablespoon powdered milk
- 1 tablespoon sugar, extra

The steps (or instructions) you must follow.

Method ◄——————————— They are in the order you do them.

1. Sift flour into a large bowl. Stir in sugar. Mix in the butter.
2. **Whisk** together water, egg, and powdered milk. Mix into flour mixture with a knife. Lightly mix in crushed pineapple.
3. Shape dough mixture into a round. Place on a well-greased baking tray. Make impressions in the dough with a knife to form 8 wedges.
4. Bake at 220°C for 25 to 30 minutes or until scone sounds hollow when tapped.
5. Sprinkle top with combined sugar and spices while hot. ◄—— Concluding step

Serve warm with butter and Mrs. Farmer's jam of choice.◄———— Concluding statement

---

1. This recipe makes _____ pineapple scones for each person to be served.

2. About how long do you estimate it would take to prepare pineapple scones? _____

3. Describe what is done when something is "whisked." _____

_____

4. Before the crushed pineapple can be used, it must be _____ .

5. It is recommended that pineapple scones be _____.

6. Name three cooking utensils required to make pineapple scones.

_____ _____ _____

7. Who or what do you think Mrs. Farmer is? _____

Name: _____ Date: _____

MAKING A PAPER GLIDER

Look at these instructions for constructing a paper glider. You will find that it will fly better than traditional paper gliders.

What you will need
- 1 sheet of letter-size paper
- 4 paper clips
- a pair of scissors

TRADITIONAL PAPER GLIDER

Directions
1. Take a sheet of letter-size paper
2. _____?
3. _____?
4. _____?
5. Make two small cuts on the fold lines in the tail.
6. Fold the flaps up.

Now it is time to test fly your glider.

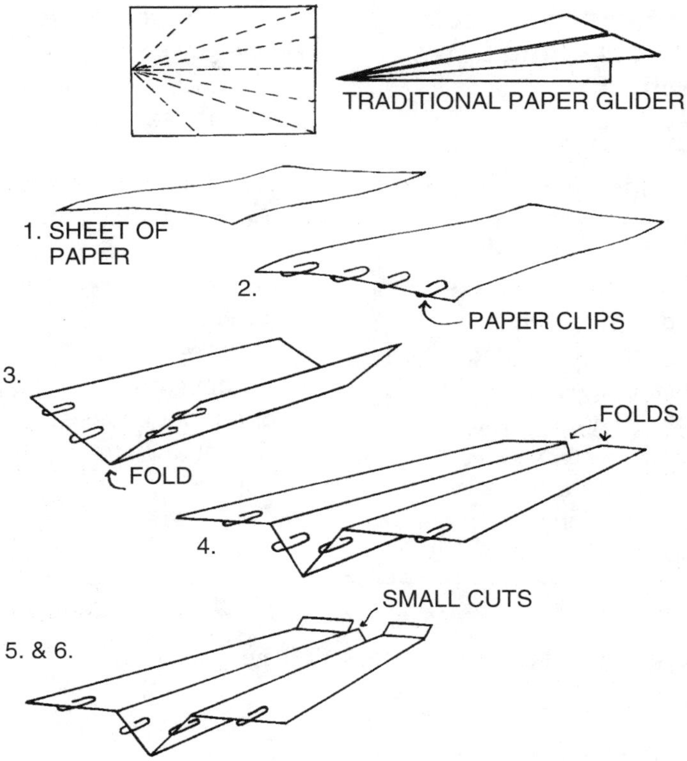

1. SHEET OF PAPER

2. PAPER CLIPS

3.

FOLD

FOLDS

4.

SMALL CUTS

5. & 6.

---

1. The word "directions" could best be replaced with the word _____ .

2. The directions are incomplete. Looking at the diagram above, complete instructions 2, 3, and 4 on these lines.

    2. _____ .

    3. _____ .

    4. _____ .

3. In the introduction, the word "traditional" could best be replaced with the word

    (A) usual.   (B) popular.   (C) historical.   (D) common.

4. What is the word for a small cut with a pair of scissors? a _____

5. The best word to replace the heading "What you will need" would be . . . (Check one box.)

    ☐ ingredients.   ☐ materials.   ☐ components.

6. What is the <u>aim</u> of these instructions? _____

7. The written instructions are easier to follow than the diagrams. ☐ True ☐ False

FOLLOWING DIRECTIONS

LAWN MOWER CARE GUIDE

These instructions differ from the earlier examples. The sequence in which owners follow the instructions/directions is not critical. The reader has some options as to how or when each instruction will be followed.

Your Keys to Trouble-Free Year-Long Lawn Mowing

Keep this guide with your mower tool kit for quick reference.

Weekly Checks
- Engine oil level.
- Fuel in tank. (Do not check while engine is running.)
- Spark plug — remove and clean.
- Clean mower deck and external fittings. (Do not use hose.)

Monthly Checks
Do weekly checks plus:
- Mower blades. (Always have a spare set of blades.)
- Oil filter.
- Air filter — clean if dirty.
- Tighten all bolts and screws.
- Grass-catcher. (Hose out accumulated build-up, clean air vents.)
- Fuel line for leaks.
- Remove build-up of grass/dirt under chassis.
- Height adjustment fittings.

Six-Monthly Checks
(or as specified by manufacturer)
- Replace oil filter and oil.
- Change air cleaner element.
- Replace spark plug.
- Check chassis for cracks.
- Throttle cable for wear.
- Replace worn blades.
- Tighten blade plate.
- Lubricate exposed parts, moving parts, and handle joints.
- Check exhaust for corrosion.

1. Which one of the following does NOT need to be checked at a weekly or monthly check?

(A) spark plug

(B) engine oil level

(C) exhaust

(D) mower blades

2. "Lubricate exposed parts, moving parts, and handle joints" means to

(A) replace damaged or worn parts.

(B) loosen all parts that have movable adjustments.

(C) apply oil to improve ease of operation and control.

(D) check for safety of any parts affected by vibrations.

3. Which of these checks is in order from most often to least often?

(A) fuel in tank, clean oil filter, replace worn blades

(B) exhaust corrosion, clean grass-catcher, remove and clean spark plug

(C) replace oil filter, clean mower deck, throttle cable for wear

(D) fuel line, tighten blade plate, remove build-up of grass under chassis

4. How often should the mower blades be changed? _____

5. The aim of these instructions is to help _____.

6. Which checklist least needs the help of a mechanic or service center? _____

Name: _____   Date: _____

SAUSAGE RECIPE

This is a recipe from the back of a curry mix box.

N E W ! **Traditional** Brand
Recipe for Curried Sausages

Use the contents of this **Traditional** pack to make a delicious meal of sausages smothered in a mild, creamy curry sauce.

Recipe Ingredients
- 8 thick sausages
- 1 onion, sliced
- 2 carrots, diced
- 1 pkt **Traditional** Curried Sausages recipe mix
- 1.5 cups water (hot for microwave)
- 2 tablespoons tomato sauce

Preparation Time: 10 minutes
Cooking time: 50–60 minutes

Directions
1. Pierce sausages several times with a fork. Place sausages, onion, and carrots in dish.

2. Combine **Traditional** recipe mix with water and tomato sauce. Pour into dish and cover.

3. Cook in gas or electric oven at 180°C for 50–60 minutes. If using a microwave, cook on HIGH for 20–25 minutes.

For a **hearty** complete meal, serve with peas and creamy mashed potatoes.

Makes four 400 g servings

---

1. What do you think the illustrations are for? _____.

2. In this recipe, the word "Traditional" refers to _____.

3. The word "hearty" in the recipe could be best replaced by

  (A) cheerful.   B) sincere.   (C) happy.   (D) satisfying.

4. Number the boxes (1, 2, 3, and 4) to show the order in which things should be done.

  ☐ Place the ingredients in a dish.   ☐ Pierce the sausages.

  ☐ Add the creamy recipe mixture.   ☐ Prepare the recipe mix.

5. How many boxes of curry mix should be used to serve 6 people? _____

6. It is not important to follow the procedure set out in the recipe. ☐ True ☐ False

7. In your opinion, who is most likely to buy this sort of product? _____

8. Briefly give reasons for your opinion in question 7. _____

9. What words in these instructions try to create the impression that this curry mix is a good product?

_____

10. What word (that doesn't have emotional qualities) could "smothered" be replaced with?

_____

Name: _____   Date: _____

INTRODUCTION

New paragraphs indicate the introduction of new circumstances or people into the writing. New paragraphs usually indicate the introduction of a change of:

- ideas or character
- place/setting/location
- speakers in conversation
- time
- action (what's happening)

Each new paragraph starts on a new line. In some writing, it is indented. The space between the paragraphs may be greater than the space between the sentences.

Paragraphs usually contain:
- a topic sentence (See Finding the Main Idea, page 17.)
- other sentences providing supporting detail
- several sentences

Single-sentence paragraphs or single-word paragraphs are used for effect (impact) or in speech/conversations. Newspapers have a convention of using single-sentence paragraphs.

Read this extract from *The Incredible Experience of Megan Kingsley* by Pamela O'Connor.

The small launch bobbed wildly in the wild choppy water, like a toy duck in a baby's bath, as the captain steered skillfully towards the rocky, forbidden cove of Stellar Island.

To the two small figures sitting in the bow, the cove appeared to have been carved out of the two sheer black cliff faces that rose straight up from the sea. The children laughed suddenly as the cold spray splashed all over them.

"Patrick and Annabel!" their mother called. "Come back here!"

The pair reluctantly left the front of the boat and clambered down the small hatch to the cabin below. Their older sister sat quietly on a bench staring stonily at the water lapping against the porthole.

"What's the matter with Megan?" asked Annabel.

"Nothing," replied their mother. "Just leave her alone."

"I'm hungry," announced Patrick. "Can we have something to eat?"

"We'll be landing in a few minutes. We'll have lunch when we get to the house." Mrs. Kingsley frowned as she looked at her elder daughter, wondering how much longer Megan could keep up this stony silence. It was so unlike her.

1. Write the number of sentences in each of these paragraphs.

a) Paragraph 1 _____   b) Paragraph 2 _____   c) Paragraph 3 _____   d) Paragraph 4 _____

2. Where is the action in paragraph 1 located? _____

3. Where does the action in paragraph 2 move to? _____

4. Paragraph 6 is a new paragraph because (Check one answer.)

☐ it describes a dramatic change in events.   ☐ it introduces a break in time.

☐ the story is getting more interesting.   ☐ there has been a change in speakers.

☐ the story has moved to a new location.

5. In your opinion, which character leaves the most unanswered questions in the reader's mind?

_____. Can you explain why? _____

6. Megan is staring stonily at the water. This means she is staring without _____.

7. Rewrite paragraph 7 in indirect speech (as it would be reported in a newspaper).

_____

Name: _____   Date: _____

MYSTERY IN MANDURAH

Reports usually use indirect speech (reported speech). Read part of the newspaper article, "Mystery in Mandurah" by Jill Burgess, again.

In March 1969, a tragedy struck when local fishermen Hugh Gill and Bevan Hahn went fishing for crayfish and were never seen again.

Resident Jim Spice could recall the day he went to meet Gill's vessel, the *Avaneta*, at the government jetty. But it was an appointment she did not keep.

Gill, 62, and Hahn, 33, were last seen shifting craypots more than 36 km off Halls Head, but an intensive search by fishermen and a coastal sweep by a flotilla of yachts returning from Bunbury failed to turn up any clues.

The weather was rough and the 22-year-old boat, previously wrecked on the entrance bar, should not have been rebuilt and certainly not have put to sea in the condition it was in.

Later, fisherman Ray Brennan discovered a number of craypots, floats, and ropes adrift in the general area of the *Avaneta*'s last sighting.

The floats were clearly marked with the vessel's number and an echo sounder revealed an object the size of the missing vessel 40 m down on the ocean bed.

Convinced it was *Avaneta*, Brennan and others marked the spot and spent precious time needed to prepare for the crayfish season guiding police and divers to the spot.

But the search was called off when police claimed their divers were not equipped to do deep dives.

Later in the year, a row was brewing as fishermen and residents claimed police were reluctant to follow a lead which could solve the disappearance.

There were conflicting opinions as to why specialist help was not obtained and the site investigated further.

According to reports, the marker flag was moved when the dive was abandoned and the spot could not later be identified.

A second theory blamed the recent Meekering earthquake, which caused tremors which set the flag adrift and shifted the vessel on the ocean bed.

The marker was eventually found miles away.

But the only clue ever to **come to light** was Gill's fishing box, found on the beach.

1. Most of the paragraphs in this article are single sentence paragraphs.   (Yes / No)

2. In two or three words describe what each of the following paragraphs is about. There may be more than one way of describing what each paragraph is about. The first one has been done for you.

   Paragraph 1: ____When it happened____   Paragraph 4: _____

   Paragraph 2: _____   Paragraph 5: _____

   Paragraph 3: _____   Paragraph 6: _____

3. Why do you think newspaper articles use one sentence paragraphs? _____

   _____

4. Rewrite the second paragraph in direct speech. (Use quotation marks.) _____

   _____

5. The phrase "came to light" could be replaced by the words "to be _____."

6. Suggest a newspaper headline suitable for the first reports of this incident, in 1969.

   _____

Name: _____   Date: _____

PARAGRAPH EXERCISES

On this page are four exercises in which you are asked to select where the paragraph breaks should be. The passages have been copied without the breaks in place. Mark a double slash (//) where one paragraph ends and a new paragraph begins.

1. Mark a double slash in three places where a new paragraph should begin. The first one has been done to help you.

Patricia Turner was born on December 2, 1939 in Marrickville, Sydney.   Her parents were living in New South Wales before she was born. // Soon after Patricia was born, she and her parents moved to an outer suburb of Brisbane.   In those days, outer suburbs were more like country towns than urban areas.   It was here she came to love the freedom rural life offered.   When she was six, she attended the local primary school.   There were less than fifty pupils enrolled at the school in those days, most of them the sons and daughters of local farmers.   Many years later she returned to the school.   As she walked in the gate, she could see the changes.   More students, more teachers, more buildings.   And she was the new principal.

2. In this excerpt from _Night of the Muttonbirds_ by Mary Small, mark a double slash in four places where new paragraphs should start. There are five paragraphs altogether.

Matthew shifted restlessly in his chair and glanced up at the schoolroom clock on the wall opposite.   Ten-thirty already!   What had happened?   Had something gone wrong?   Today was mail day but the plane was later than usual, and on this of all days when his grandmother, Annie, was returning from hospital in Tasmania.   In nervous anticipation he sat staring out of the window, chewing his fingernails, listening, waiting.   "Matthew!" Mr. Trent's voice was sharp.   Matthew glanced at him in exasperation, sighed and made a half-hearted attempt to concentrate on the subject in front of him.   Then, to his enormous relief, he heard it, at first indistinct but unmistakable.   The low steady drone of an aircraft approaching.   He stood up pushing his books aside.   "Matthew!   Sit down!"   "It's coming," said Matthew.   "The plane, I mean. Mr. Greg's coming."

3. In this excerpt from a newspaper, mark five places where new paragraphs should start.

Students threatened with expulsion or suspension from school will now have the opportunity to have their side of the argument heard before a special "education" judge.   The Department of Education has brought in guidelines which will give a student a fair hearing in cases where the student feels he or she has not been treated fairly.   A parent group from the north coast of NSW said that this change was long overdue. However, groups supporting greater discipline in schools disagree, saying that students now have too many rights and genuine learners are being disadvantaged.   Ms. Kathy Kane, spokesperson for the Department, said she welcomed the change.   The new guidelines will come into effect from the beginning of the new school year.

4. In this short conversation, mark three places where new paragraphs should start.

"I heard that, Michelle!" said Ms. Wright.   "Stand up!"   "Who me?"   I tried to look innocent.   "I didn't say anything!"   Ms. Wright sighed.   She looked up at the ceiling then back at me.   "It was a ventriloquist, was it?"   I really don't like those sorts of questions.   Agree, and you are being rude.   Disagree, and you get laughed at by the class.

Name: _____   Date: _____

INTRODUCTION

Almost without being aware of it, we are bombarded with persuasive messages every day. You cannot watch television, listen to the radio, or read a magazine without being confronted with advertisements which are trying to get you to choose a particular product or service.

But there are other ways people use persuasion. Your school friends may try to persuade you to join them in an after-school activity. Another student may try to persuade you that he or she is the best person for class president. These people are trying to persuade you to think or act in a particular way.

Persuasive writing has some special features:
- it tries to attract (and hold) the reader's attention
- it may use a mixture of logical and emotional language
- it sounds convincing (as if the writer is an expert) and often has an element of urgency
- it often appears to address the reader/listener in a personal way

Read this advertisement from a tourist magazine.

The world's most exciting Jet Boat ride!
Rapid Ride

Rapid Ride jets bring blood-pumping excitement to your vacation. The year-round sunshine makes Coral Harbor a great place to experience the exhilarating, yet safe, Rapid Ride Jet Fly-Over. The unbelievable speed and maneuverability of the jet boats will thrill you as you blast along narrow gorges, over tumbling white rapids, and through mangrove tunnels as **you** race for the coast.

Join over two million people who have had this experience of a lifetime. Make it a part of **your** Coral Harbor vacation.

During April, Kids are free on **Rapid Ride** jets.
One child per full-fare paying adult on **Rapid Ride** jet rides for **FREE!**

Conditions apply:
- child must be aged between 5 and 15
- offer only valid Mon to Thurs (school term only)
- offer not valid on school holidays.

Ride the rapids with **Rapid Ride**
For further information, call Laura at
1-800-200-2002 between 9 A.M. and 5 P.M.

LEARNING POINTS
- Speaks to the reader directly by using the words *your* and *you*.
- Attracts the reader's attention with a picture and large type for the heading.
- This ad appeals to the emotions more than to common sense (logic).
- The ad gives the impression that this could be happening for you right now, just by (your parents) making the right decision.
- The ad is loaded with colorful words: "blood-pumping," "exhilarating," "thrill," "blast."
- "You" see yourself (male or female) being part of the ride.
- Being part of two million is an extra incentive—it makes you feel you've been part of a popular event.
- Makes use of a slogan.
- Concluding statement (information available).

1. Who are you expected to think of instead of the people in the jet boat? _____

2. What is the slogan used by Rapid Ride? _____

3. This ad emphasizes a need to act without too much delay. ☐ True ☐ False

4. What do you think will be the effect of the free offer? _____

5. As two million people have enjoyed this ride, is it assumed that you will also? (**Yes** / **No**)

6. Give two colorful words used in the ad. _____ _____

EARTH FIRST

David Bowden and Jenny Dibley looked at how people are influenced by persuasive advertising.

Why Do We Consume So Much?

Many of us are starting to ask the question: "Why do I buy so many things?" Can you think back to toys that you have owned? What has happened to them? What about all your friend's toys? Some of them have ended up in the local trash bin, and many of your toys have not been biodegradable. Think about how much more waste you and your friends will contribute over the next ten years.

Companies have employed many people and spent millions of dollars on advertising creating new ways to sell products. Some methods used to entice consumers are listed below.

Time-Saving Devices

Disposable items have become popular in the past twenty years. They are products we use only once, or a few times, then throw away. These disposable products include drink and food containers, razors, tissues, pens, and cameras. Disposable products are convenient for busy families. They have been designed to save time for our fast-moving society.

Many disposable products are used at fast-food places. When we order a meal, it sometimes comes in a polystyrene container, with paper napkins, plastic eating utensils, and a tray with a paper placemat. Our drinks are served in plastic cups, and we drink them through a plastic straw. There is often more packaging than food.

Extra, Extra!

It is common practice to produce items that require accessories that make them seem complete. For example, a doll may have accessories, such as clothing, which are sold separately. Accessories cost more money, and advertisements for them are designed to make us feel that our original purchase is incomplete.

Sale Time

Bargain sales are a great way to tempt consumers. Most shops have sales regularly, to move old or discontinued stock. Are there really bargains in these shops, or is it just a way to get you to buy the products even if you don't need them?

Most forms of advertising follow a simple format. Advertisements promote a way of life that is presented as ideal. People in advertisements are usually attractive, happy, own expensive cars and houses, and generally promote a high standard of living. Is this really how most people live?

"Hurry Before They All Run Out!"

There are many ways of persuading us to consume. Sometimes we shop to the sound of a voice telling us we can get "two for the price of one!" or "hurry before they all run out." We are often told that "an offer like this will never be repeated." The implication is that we cannot live without these products.

---

1. People in ads are usually (**aged   pleasant   male   wealthy   uncooperative**). (Circle two answers.)

2. The writers have included questions in the passage. These questions are meant to

   (A)   raise issues that need answers.   (B)   develop consumer/reader awareness.

   (C)   be answered by the reader.   (D)   help readers with their research.

3. Of the following goods, which is the most likely to use the least advertising for extras?

   ☐ bread   ☐ four-wheel drive   ☐ computer   ☐ swimming pool

4. Name one advertising technique from the article above. _____

5. Name one item that has become disposable in recent years. _____

6. Name a toy that you once owned that didn't live up to its TV image. _____

7. What do most ads promote? _____

Name: _____   Date: _____

THE YEAR 2000 PROBLEM

Not all persuasive writing uses techniques that appeal to the reader's emotions, ego, or prestige. Some writing tries to persuade us to act or think in a particular way by appealing to our reasoning. Read the following excerpt—it was printed just after the impact of the Millennium Bug was being understood.

Will Your Business Survive the Year 2000?

In the early days of computing, machines were large and memory space was limited. To conserve as much memory as possible, programmers stored dates only using the last two digits of the year. At the time, no one imagined that those same programs would still be in use at the end of the century. More than forty years later the two-digit date field remains an industry standard. The transition to a new year is a logical forward motion—97 becomes 98 and 98 becomes 99. The digits 99 are computed as 1999, and the roll over to 00 will be computed as 1900—**a giant leap backward in time!**

Left unchecked, most computer systems, unable to bridge this gap in their internal logic, will at the stroke of midnight on December 31, 1999, shut down, reject new data, or begin making calculations that can create chaos in a business or organization.

This seemingly minor problem has the potential to cripple accounting systems, payroll systems, and long term timetables, **to name just a few**.

The belief that the Year 2000 problem is entirely a mainframe issue is a myth. Most personal computers, network systems, and software applications are affected by the Year 2000 problem. In fact, the Year 2000 glitch could disable embedded chip computer systems that operate elevators, air-cooling systems, security systems, and telephone-message centers.

A quick check around many homes will give an insight as to how many of our everyday household appliances use clocks. The video recorder, cameras, the stove, and the microwave quickly come to mind. After January 2000 we will know just how well people reacted to warnings about the Millennium Bug.

The clock is ticking.

1. The writer of the article most likely believes that
   (A) it is too late to combat the Millennium Bug.
   (B) more people will be affected than is generally realized.
   (C) the Millennium Bug is mainly a mainframe issue.
   (D) programmers of the first computers were concerned about problems in memory availability.

2. In your opinion, the writer appeals least to the reader's
   (A) logic.   (B) sense of justice.   (C) financial concerns.   (D) fears.

3. Why is the recording of the Year 2000 as 00 called "a giant leap backward in time"?

   _____

4. According to the article, the non-scientific reader can check the claims made by the writer by

   _____.

5. This article would most likely appear in a
   (A) research journal.   (B) home entertainment guide.
   (C) computer manual.   (D) business magazine.

6. This article is mostly based upon (fact   opinion). (Circle one answer.)

7. What is the effect of the last sentence—"The clock is ticking."? _____

8. What is the effect of the phrase "to name just a few"? _____

Name: _____   Date: _____

INTRODUCTION

Facts and opinions are part of our everyday speech and writing. It is important to know when someone is using an argument based on their opinion to persuade you to believe or do something. (See Recognizing Persuasion, page 47, and Finding the Facts, page 11.) A **fact** is something that everyone agrees with. It can usually be proven either by observation or written records. The wording of facts is usually precise. We are often given the source of facts. An **opinion** is a particular viewpoint of the writer or speaker. An opinion can be as follows:

- be personal.
- be used to influence (or convince) the reader or listener with emotional language.
- provide suggestions on courses of action (what to do).

Read this extract.

> There are now less than 300 elephants left in lower sections of the valley. These beautiful animals once roamed free across the valley right up to the low foothills of the western range. The uncontrolled slaughter of the elephant herds is to be deplored.

Fact: There are now less than 300 elephants left in lower sections of the valley. This could be proved by doing a count, doing some research, and comparing elephant populations over a period of time.
Opinion: These beautiful animals—some people may think they are beautiful but it cannot be proved. It is quite possible many people may have a different opinion.

In opinionative writing, the writer expresses a judgment, may make recommendations, and has a stated point of view.

> I think all children should play sports. It keeps them healthy, and it makes them better people. We all respect our famous sportspeople.
>
> If children don't play sports, they grow up lazy and disinterested in life. As they get older, they become unfit and have to have medical treatment which is unfair to other members of their families.
>
> The council should spend more money on building pools and sports grounds.

Read the passage above. In this passage, it is quite easy to determine the opinions held by the writer.

1. How would you describe the writer's opinion on sports? _____

2. What are the first words that warn the reader that this writing is opinion? _____

Read this extract adapted from *Shaping the News* by John D. Fitzgerald.

> Most people enjoy reading about crime, especially violent crime. Stories about bombings, murders, armed robberies that involve large sums of money, and serious assaults attract readers, especially if they are local events.
>
> An unusual crime is highly newsworthy. Once it was rare for bank robberies to occur and when they did they were reported in detail. Now there are many more robberies, and they tend to be reported in much less detail.
>
> The ultimate act of violent conflict is war between nations. This should be newsworthy. However, unless our country or its friends are involved, the news reports of the war are only brief.

3. Most people enjoy reading about crime, especially violent crime. (fact   opinion)

4. An unusual crime is highly newsworthy. (fact   opinion)

5. Once it was rare for bank robberies to occur. (fact   opinion)

6. Most of the information in the extract is fact. (True / False)

7. What does the writer want the reader to react to? _____

SHOPPING CARTS

from "Why Shopping Trips End in Tears for Kids" by Vincent Kiernan

Read the magazine article on this page and answer the questions on fact and opinion.

Supermarket carts are responsible for injuring more than 26,000 American children each year, and should be redesigned to make them more stable, say four pediatricians from Ohio State University College of Medicine.

"Shopping carts are not designed for the safe transport of children," the doctors say in the current issue of the *Archives of Pediatric Medicine*.

Today's carts have a narrow wheel base and are prone to tip over. The child's seat, located high on the cart, gives the cart a high center of gravity, making it even more likely to tip, say the researchers. Strapping children in is no protection if the cart is upset.

So the pediatricians would like to see the shopping carts **redesigned** with the wheels positioned further apart. And they **think** the child should ride in a separate carrier attached to the cart, and closer to the ground.

According to government statistics, some 26,700 children were taken to hospitals for emergency treatment after cart accidents in 1992. About 43% of them suffered contusions or abrasions. Another 25% had cuts. But 6% had concussions and 2% had broken bones.

Serious injuries do happen. During the three-year period, the team estimates that about 2,000 children had to be kept in the hospital because of fractures, concussions, and internal injuries.

Poor supervision by parents may be as much to **blame** for the accidents as poor cart design: a separate survey has shown that 80% of parents leave their child unattended at least once while they search the supermarket shelves.

The pediatricians, however, **suggest** that it is probably easier to redesign the cart than to change the shopping habits of millions of parents.

1. Referring to the above article, check the boxes that express *opinions*.

   ☐ Supermarket carts are responsible for injuring more than 26,000 American children.

   ☐ Poor supervision by parents may be as much to blame for the accidents.

   ☐ Children should ride in a separate carrier.

   ☐ Today's carts have a narrow wheel base.

2. This report contains research *facts*, but much of the text is *opinion*.   ☐ True   ☐ False

3. Check the boxes which are *facts* taken from the above passage.

   ☐ A separate survey has shown that 80% of parents leave their child unattended.

   ☐ It is probably easier to redesign the cart than to change shopping habits.

   ☐ They [pediatricians] think the child should be closer to the ground.

   ☐ The child's seat, located high on the cart, gives the cart a high center of gravity.

4. Which words warn the reader that the information is probably an opinion? (Check one or more boxes.)

   ☐ think   ☐ redesigned   ☐ suggest   ☐ blame

5. It is a *fact* that parents' shopping habits cannot be changed.   ☐ True   ☐ False

6. Because the writer refers to professional sources, the reader is likely to _____ the article.

7. The writer expresses a firm view on cart safety.   ☐ True   ☐ False

Name: _____   Date: _____

GLOBAL WARMING

from *Technology for the Environment* by Mike Callaghan and Peter Knapp

The Earth's climate has changed over millions of years. Places that were once rainforests are now deserts; places which are now on the tops of mountains, hundreds of kilometers from the sea, were once on the ocean floor. Sometimes the climatic changes have been small and could only be noticed by sensitive scientific instruments. At other times, they have been extreme. The ice ages are an example of climatic change. Ice from the polar regions expanded, reaching areas thousands of kilometers away. During the last ice age, humans had to greatly change their lifestyles. They used technology such as fire, the ability to make clothing, and shelter, and most importantly, the capacity to think and solve problems to ensure their survival. Animals that could not use technology or move to warmer regions died as the climate changed.

For millions of years climatic changes were due to natural causes rather than the activities of human beings. However, since the Industrial Revolution over 200 years ago, the actions of people and their use of machines has had a greater and greater effect on the world's climate. Perhaps their greatest influence has been the greenhouse effect.

The amount of greenhouse gases released into the atmosphere since the Industrial Revolution has increased hugely. This is because of the increased use of cars, the clearing and burning of forests, the way people use the planet for food production, and the way people live, using appliances such as air-conditioners and heaters. The greenhouse gases that are the result of human activities rise into the atmosphere and act like a blanket to decrease the amount of radiated heat.

In Australia, scientists predict that there will be a rise in the sea levels with more floods and droughts, and the snowline in the snow field of NSW and Victoria will recede. Parts of inland Australia will receive more rainfall and the cyclone belt of Northern Australia will move further south. There is also the prediction that these changes will affect Australia's energy resources, agriculture, and tourist industries. The transport we use, the way we communicate, and even our health may be affected.

1. Which of the following statements is an *opinion* taken from the article?

   (A) The amount of greenhouse gases released into the atmosphere since the Industrial Revolution has increased hugely.

   (B) The Earth's climate has changed over millions of years.

   (C) The way we communicate and even our health may be affected.

   (D) The ice ages are an example of climatic change.

2. This article mainly uses (fact   opinion) to convince readers they should be more concerned about the environment. (Circle one answer.)

3. In your opinion, if this article was in a newspaper, would it be on the front page? _____

4. Give a reason for your opinion. _____

5. According to the article, the most important factor contributing to global warming is natural climatic change.   ☐ True   ☐ False

6. Global warming most likely began

   (A) when cave people began using fire.

   (B) with the invention of the motor car.

   (C) with the start of the Industrial Revolution.

   (D) when people started to use such appliances as air conditioners.

7. According to the article, how do people differ from other animals? _____

INTRODUCTION

When we say something is **relevant**, we are saying it is appropriate or of some importance. It has some significance. If it is **irrelevant**, then it is the opposite. It is inappropriate, unimportant, or insignificant. When writing, especially school assignments, only include material relevant to the topic.

It is also important to understand the relevance of information when involved in research at school. It is important to know what is relevant and what is irrelevant when we make plans to undertake certain tasks. When writing fiction (creative writing), it is important to recognize if the information is relevant to your story. Irrelevant information will make your story less appealing to the reader.

Read these instructions for playing the game *Snakes and Ladders*.

TO START THE GAME	TO CONTINUE THE GAME
• Put one counter for each player on **START**. • Sometimes the counters are called "men." • To begin playing, each player must first roll a six on the die. • Once the player gets a six, he or she rolls the die again and then moves his or her counter the number of places shown on the die.	• Players take turns in a clockwise direction. • If a counter lands on the bottom of a ladder, the player moves the counter to the top of the ladder. • If a counter lands on a snake's head, the player moves the counter to the bottom of snake's tail. • The winner is the first person to reach **FINISH**.

1. Highlight the point which has the least to do with playing *Snakes and Ladders*.

Read part of the article "Warbirds Over Wanaka" by Shiri Gounder.

Wanaka is a scenic little town about 80 km north-west of Queenstown in New Zealand. It stays fairly dry and sunny, and despite the snow-capped peaks in the distance, temperatures remain mild. Wanaka is popular with tourists and seems to have a disproportionate number of hotels and motels.

Every two years, though, over the long Easter weekend, Wanaka's normal influx of visitors positively explodes; 75,000 people drawn by a three-day air show billed as "Warbirds over Wanaka."

Aviation buffs make up most of the crowd, but the display of ex-military vehicles, vintage motorcycles, farm machinery, and antique fire engines has a certain appeal as well.

On the ground the vintage aircraft look spectacular. In the air, they're even more awesome, with aerial flying and stunt displays performed by the RNZAF Red Checkers and the Roaring Forties Harvard aerobatic teams.

2. If you wanted to see the air show, which one of the following facts would be <u>least relevant</u>?

(A) The air show is on the Easter weekend, every two years.
(B) From Wanaka, snow-capped mountains can be seen.
(C) Stunt flying is part of the Wanaka air show.
(D) Most visitors are interested in the vintage aircraft.

3. Select the most <u>relevant</u> information to illustrate the popularity of the air show.

The Wanaka air show's success can best be judged by (the size of the crowd   the weather in Wanaka   the number of hotels). (Circle one answer.)

4. The number of hotels in Wanaka is a direct result of the air show.   ☐ True   ☐ False

5. When writing a review on the air show, the size of Wanaka is vital.   ☐ True   ☐ False

TAKING BETTER PHOTOS

Important Tips for Better Flash Photos

1. Don't stand too far back from your subject. The flash on most cameras will not effectively cover any subject over three meters away. Even in non-flash photos, many photographers stand too far away from their subjects. This results in small subjects surrounded by great areas of unimportant background.

2. Watch the background to ensure there are no mirrors or shiny surfaces to bounce the flash back to the camera lens.

3. When taking pictures of people, ask them not to look into the lens but at a point over your shoulder. Otherwise there is a good chance that the flash will reflect from the backs of their pupils and they will end up with red eyes in the photo. Models 3X00 and 3X01 have a setting to reduce the red-eye effect.

4. Try to give the subjects an interesting background. If there is nothing for two meters behind the subject, the background will come out black or very dark. Of course, you don't want a cluttered background that distracts from your subject.

5. If taking a picture of a baby, make sure the room is as light as possible so that the flash does not hurt his or her eyes.

Advice for Action Photographers

Action coming straight at the camera does not require a very fast shutter speed, whereas a subject passing quickly across the front of the lens requires a much faster shutter speed.

When your subject is moving fast, there is no time to focus your camera correctly. It is best to anticipate where the action will be and pre-focus on something in that area. You may have to use manual override if you have chosen the autofocus feature in our camera range.

When shooting subjects racing across the lens, a very fast shutter speed could freeze the action and lose the idea of speed. For a better action shot, use a pan action. Swing the camera in a smooth sweep to keep the subject in the center of the viewfinder, and click. The subject will be in sharp focus but the background will be blurred to give a convincing feeling of speed.

---

1. In Point 1, "Important Tips for Better Flash Photos," highlight (or underline) any tip that is <u>irrelevant</u> to a photographer using a flash.

2. A blurred background can add to the impact of a photo if

   ☐ the person being photographed is looking at the camera.   ☐ it is a shot of a newborn baby.

   ☐ the subject is well over three meters away.   ☐ it is an action shot.

3. Which of these conditions is most <u>relevant</u> when taking flash photos of new babies?

   (A) Ensuring there are no mirrors or shiny surfaces in the background.

   (B) Anticipating where the action will be and pre-focusing on that area.

   (C) Ensuring the subject is looking over the photographer's shoulder.

   (D) Making sure the room is as light as possible.

4. If the background is unimportant, how far should it be behind the subject? _____

5. What do you consider the most relevant factor when taking good action shots?

   _____

6. What point is most relevant to you if you wanted to improve your flash photos? _____

7. When taking action photos, it is best to focus on the subject.   ☐ True   ☐ False

Name: _____ Date: _____

INTRODUCTION

Most factual books have a **table of contents**. This is found in the front of the book, usually within the first few pages. A table of contents is a quick reference which helps readers find the main sections of the book. Some books are broken up into major chapters or topics, and within each chapter, section, or subject area there are sub-sections.

Books of fiction may also have a table of contents. These give the chapter pages or, if it is a book of many works (an anthology), the page on which individual stories, plays, or poems are located.

Here is a table of contents from *Touch and Feeling* by Robert Royston.

Table of Contents

INTRODUCTION	5
1 FEELINGS	7–9
What touch tells us	7–8
Sensitive and insensitive	9
2 HOW TOUCH WORKS	10–15
The skin	10–11
Reacting to touch	12–13
Inside the body	14–15
3 PRESSURE AND TOUCH	16–19
Exploring touch	16–17
Using and losing touch	18–19
4 HOT AND COLD	20–25
Exploring temperature	20–21
Keeping cool and	
keeping warm	22–23
Too much heat or cold	24–25
5 FEELING PAIN	26–29
Itching, tickling, or hurting	26–27
Painkillers	28–29
6 GLOSSARY	30
7 BIBLIOGRAPHY	30
INDEX	31

Page numbers are often in columns. In some books they are at the end of the text.

Main headings/Chapters (in capitals)

Sub-headings (in lower case)

Suggested reading (Books to Read) includes other books on the same topic.

The **glossary** is an explanation of unusual words or phrases used in the book. It is in alphabetical order.

The **index** is an alphabetical list of the many topics covered in the book with their page numbers. (See page 57.)

A **bibliography** is a list of books referred to in the text.

1. On what pages would you find information about controlling pain? _____

2. The bibliography is on page 30. ☐ True ☐ False

3. There are five chapters in the book. The shortest of these is _____.

4. The meaning of the word "angina" would most likely be found in the _____.

5. I want to find out about bathing a baby. What pages might give some information? _____

6. The word "acupuncture" is used in the book. Where would I first look to find all references to

   "acupuncture" in the book? _____.

7. What one word could be used to replace "sensitive and insensitive"? _____

Name: _____   Date: _____

THE AGE OF DINOSAURS IN AUSTRALIA

from a book by by Dr. Tim Flannery & Paula Kendall

1. On what page will the reader find information about Lightning Ridge? _____

2. Which section is the longest section in the book? _____

3. In which section could the reader get the names of some other books on dinosaurs?

_____

4. Fossils are referred to in the book. Where would I first look to find all references to fossils?

_____

5. To find the meaning of the word "vertebra," you would use the index.   ☐ True   ☐ False

6. There are two topics on page 55.   ☐ True   ☐ False

7. The authors referred to other books when compiling their book.   ☐ True   ☐ False

8. This book is mainly about dinosaurs in _____.

9. Which is the better title for the book with this table of contents? (Check one answer.)

☐   The Age of Dinosaurs in Australia   ☐   Prehistoric Terrors of Australia

Name: _____ Date: _____

INTRODUCTION

Many factual books have indexes. They are found at the back of the book. An **index** is a quick reference which helps readers find the information in a book that is not easily found using the table of contents. The index items are listed alphabetically and give one or more pages where information may be found. References longer than one page are shown by using a hyphen or a dash (e.g., 34–37).

One of the main skills in using an index is finding the right reference word. If you wanted to find information on rainfall, you might have to look under the entry for weather. If you don't find what you are looking for the first time, try some other possibilities.

Use the index from *Technology for the Environment* by Mike Callaghan & Peter Knapp to answer the questions below.

Index

Acid rain, 12–13
Antarctica, 17, 42
Arctic, 17, 42

Chernobyl, 13
chlorofluorocarbons (CFCs), 44–49
climate, 15–22

electricity, 7, 10
energy supply systems, 7
environmental pollution, 11–13

feral animals, 40–41
fossil fuels, 9–10
fuel cells, 9

global warming, 16–22
greenhouse effect, 19

greenhouse gases, 16, 19–20, 42

incineration, 26, 27, 30
Industrial Revolution, 19
irrigation, 36–37, 41

land degradation, 33–41
landfill, 26–27, 30–31

nuclear energy, 4, 9, 13

oxygen, 43–44
ozone layer, 42–46, 48

radioactive gases, 13
recycling, 32

satellites, 21
sewage, 27–30

soil, 18, 33–41, 47
  acidity, 35, 39
  contamination, 35, 39
  erosion, 35–36
  salinity, 35, 37–38
  structure, 35, 38
solar energy, 22

ultraviolet rays, 43, 45, 47

waste, 23–32
  disposal, 25–26
  domestic, 23
  hazardous, 24, 30–32
  industrial, 23
  liquid, 23–25, 27, 31
  management, 23–32
  solids, 23–27, 30
  toxic, 11, 23, 31–32
watertable, 38

1. On what pages would you find information on animals that are feral? _____

2. How many different references are there to ozone layer in the index? _____

3. If you wanted to find out about recycled paper, you would look under _____.

4. How many different types of waste are referred to in the book? _____

5. To find out about droughts, you will have to look under _____ .

6. To find information on types of energy, what is one entry I could try? _____

7. The <u>major</u> entry for greenhouse gases commences on page (16 19 20 42). (Circle one answer.)

8. Under which subject area would you find the word "salinity"? (Check one box.)

☐ waste ☐ soil ☐ sewage

Name: _____   Date: _____

SHAPING THE NEWS
by John D. Fitzgerald

Indexes also have their own shortcuts. To save space, the main entry may not be repeated (a bit like in a dictionary). If you wanted to find out about writing, you may have to decide what sort of writing—writing radio news or writing television news. Such sub-entries are often slightly indented. When the word "the" is part of a name or title, it is usually placed last in an index entry. (See "Ashes, The" below.) Numbers in italics refer to illustrations.

Index

ABC radio, 34
   news, 6
ABC TV, 18
   news, 27
accuracy of media, 39
Age, The, 6
America's Cup, 7
Ash Wednesday 1983, 29–30
Ashes, The, *7*

Berlin Wall, *8*
BHP, 35

Cave, Peter, 29
Channel Nine, *19*, 26–27
Channel Ten Eyewitness News, 27
conflict, 3, 39
Cottee, Kay, 7
court cases, 20
crime, 4
current affairs, 33

D-cart technology, 35
Delahunty, Mary, *21*, 27

Gulf War, *29*

Henderson, Brian, *26–27*
Herald-Sun, News-Pictorial, 11
human interest, 6

Johnston, David, 27

Koori viewpoints, *14*
Kostakidis, Mary, *17*, 22
Koval, Ramona, 33–34

logging of forests, 33

media sources, 40
Morecroft, Richard, *23*
Murphy, Paul, *17*
Murray, Les, *17*

Newcastle, NSW, *5*, 14
newspapers, 2–14
   timing of news, 40

newsworthiness, 3–8, 39–40
   variations on, 8
Nicoll, Murray, *30*
Nyngan, NSW, *5*, 14

oddities, *6*
outstanding feats, 6–7

photographs, newspaper, 13–15
pictures, 24–25
   television, 17–18

radio, 28–38
   first with news, 40

form of the news, 34–37
image of the news, 38
transitions in, 35
Rainbow Warrior, *8*, 36, 37

SBS television, 17–18, *26*
Scott, James, 7
selection of news, 33–34
sound, 24–25
Supreme Court, NSW, 20

television
   forms of news, 18–25
   image of news, 26–27
   time limits on, 21–22
   timing of news, 40
   transitions in news reports, 22
tragedy, 5

unusual, the, 6

werewolf, 6
Western Odyssey, 36, 37
who-what-where-when, 10
writing
   newspaper reports, 9–13
   radio news, 35–37
   television news, 23

Yugoslavia, *3*, *14*

1. On what page would you find information about "The Age"? _____

2. If I looked up "Yugoslavia" and went to page 14, what should I find? _____

3. The entry on "pictures" commences on page 24 and finishes on page _____.

4. What entry word should you look up to find information on Peter Cave? _____

5. The entries in this index are arranged in . . . (Check one box.)

   ☐ order of importance   ☐ order of appearance in the book.   ☐ alphabetical order.

6. An illustration for the entry "werewolf" is on page 6.   ☐ True   ☐ False

7. The entry, "The Ashes," comes before the entry, "Les Murray."   ☐ True   ☐ False

8. In the book, radio is a more important topic than crime because _____.

9. There (is one   are two) references in the index to ABC TV. (Circle one answer.)

Name: _____   Date: _____

INTRODUCTION

A **schedule** is a list of events according to time. Schedules play an important part in our lives. Some of us use schedules for bus or train travel. We have schedules at school and schedules for sports. The program for the school concert is a type of schedule.

Without schedules we could be late for school! Schedules help us to keep our lives in order. A TV guide is a list of programs arranged according to the time when they are screened. Use this excerpt from a TV guide to answer the questions below.

SATURDAY December 2			Western Herald (free TV guide)				
WBN		**WTV**		**WON**		**WSB**	
Noon	Sports Scene (includes clips from today's athletics, tennis, golf, bowls, horse racing, and motor sports)	Noon	MOVIE Secret Orders **G**	Noon	International Sports (discussion panel)	Noon	Rage On (music)
		2:00	Regional Athletics Championships (Nowra hosts the third regional championships.)	1:00	Karaoke Craze **Rpt**	1:00	Report from Britain **Rpt**
				1:35	Due South **G** (Britton follows the trails of Antarctic adventurers.)		
3:00	News Update					2:30	Sky Divers **G**
3:10	Sports Scene (cont.)			3:00	Basketball Guide	3:00	Golf Courses in Scotland
		3:45	MOVIE Amazon Ordeal (91) **Rpt G**	3:30	MOVIE Last Man Out (75) **Rpt G**	4:00	Theater Review
5:00	News and Weather			5:00	Latest in Sports	5:00	Pet Vet Hotline
5:30	Good Cooking	5:30	News and Weather			5:30	Cartoon Fun
		6:00	Talking of Sport	6:00	News at 6	6:30	News and Weather
6:30	Park Ranger **Rpt**	6:30	Holiday Time	6:30	Reward: Police Files	7:00	Don't Stop Now! **G**
7:30	Murder Squad	7:30	Better Gardens **G**	7:30	MOVIE The Game	7:30	Tourist Track **G**
8:30	Art News - Latest Exhibitions **M**	8:30	Beach Beat **PG** (Sally leaves Brett.)		**Rpt G**	8:30	MOVIE: Comet (Italy 96) **M S**
Programs	**G** - General		**PG** - Parent guidance		**M** - Mature audience		
	R - Adult		**Rpt** - Repeat		**S** - Subtitles		

1. Which channel has news at 5 P.M.? _____ 2. How long is <u>Due South</u> on WON? _____

3. Is <u>Art News</u> suitable for children? _____ 4. Which channel has the most sports? _____

5. What does **PG** stand for? _____ 6. When do **M** rated shows begin? _____

7. Which program provides subtitles? _____ .

8. I have a 90 minute videotape. Can I fully record the movie <u>Amazon Ordeal</u>? _____

9. If I watched <u>Reward: Police Files</u>, I would miss <u>Don't Stop Now!</u> ☐ True ☐ False

10. The last half-hour evening news report is on at 6:00. ☐ True ☐ False

11. How long is <u>Sports Scene</u> on WBN? _____

12. What program might I watch if I was interested in motor sports? _____

13. How much does this TV guide cost? _____

14. Which channel appears to best cater to the interests of young children? _____

15. Which movie is not suitable for children? _____

BEGA VALLEY MOBILE LIBRARY SERVICE

In many rural areas the library becomes mobile. The local town library uses a van to take library services to outlying areas. This three-month schedule for towns in the Bega Valley was reproduced in the local newspaper. There are no library services on public holidays (* indicates a public holiday).

Place/Town	Location	Time	Day	Sept	Oct	Nov
Merimbula	Smarties Child Care	2:30 – 3:15	Fri	11	2, 3	13
Nethercote	Near bridge	1:00 – 1:30	Mon	14	26*	16
Pambula	Pre-school	10:00 – 10:45	Fri	7, 28	19	9, 30
	Beach	1:15 – 2:45	Thu	18	9, 30	20
	Toalla Rd	3:00 – 3:45	Wed	18	9, 30	20
	Pambula Public School	11:30 – 12:15	Fri	18	9, 30	20
Quaama	Near school	1:00 – 2:30	Thu	10	1, 22	12, 16
Rocky Hall	Community hall	10:15 – 12:00	Wed	16	7, 28	18
South Pambula	Near the Grange	11:45 – 12:30	Mon	7, 28	19	9, 30
Tanja	Near school	11:15 – 12:15	Tue	15	6, 27	17
Tathra	Pre-school	10:00 – 10:45	Tue	15	6, 27	17
	Beach car park	1:15 – 3:15	Tue	15	6, 27	17
	Retirement village	10:00 – 11:00	Tue	8, 29	20	10
	Public School	12:45 – 2:30	Tue	8, 29	20	10
Towamba	Near school	12:30 – 2:15	Fri	4, 25	16	6, 27
Tura Beach	Near pre-school	1:00 – 3:00	Tue	1, 22	13	3, 24
		11:30 – 1:30	Fri	11	2, 23	13
Wandella	Community hall	1:45 – 2:45	Wed	2, 23	14	4, 25
Wolumba	Near school	1:00 – 12:00	Tue	1, 22	13	3, 24
Womboyn	General store	2:30 – 4:30	Mon	14	26*	16
Wyndham	Public School	1:00 – 3:00	Wed	9, 16, 30	7, 21, 28	11, 18
Yowrie	Sutherland Rd	11:45 – 12:45	Wed	2, 23	14	4, 25

1. On what day does the mobile van visit Tathra Pre-school? _____

2. This schedule is organized

    (A) in a chronological order of the times and dates various places are visited.

    (B) according to the size of community visited by the mobile van.

    (C) considering the distance the community is from Bega.

    (D) in alphabetical order of the communities.

3. Womboyn is a small community. Which fact supports this statement?

    (A) the number of visits it has each month   (B) Womboyn's position on the list

    (C) the place where the van provides its services   (D) the time of the day for visits by the van

4. The mobile library van goes to three public schools. They are:

    1. _____   2. _____   3. _____

5. How many hours is the mobile library van in Wyndham in October? _____

6. The mobile van will not make any visits on October 26. Why? _____

7. Visits to Tathra Public School and Tathra Pre-school are on the same weekday. ☐ True ☐ False

8. Which community has the last library visit in September? _____

Name: _____   Date: _____

INTRODUCTION

We usually think of atlases when we think of **maps**. But maps can be found in many other places. Most people who live in big cities use a street directory. People who do a lot of traveling might use a road map. People interested in the universe might use a star map. When studying maps, we are usually interested in distance and direction.

The Oaks — Town and locality map

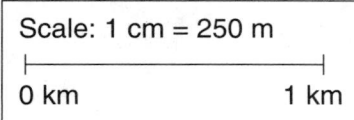

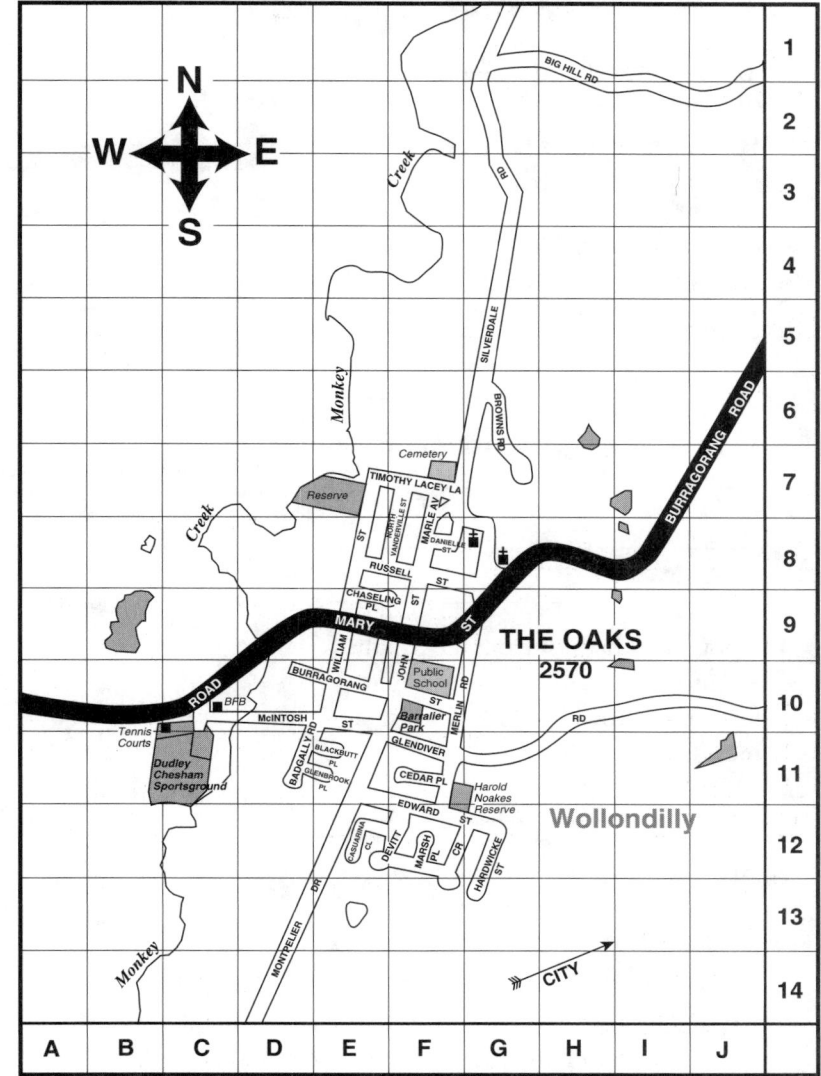

1. To go to the City from The Oaks you would have to travel to the
   - (A) west.
   - (B) north.
   - (C) northeast.
   - (D) southwest.

2. The coordinates for the public school are
   - (A) E 10.
   - (B) F 9.
   - (C) G 11.
   - (D) F 10.

3. The cemetery is at the corner of
   - (A) Silverdale Rd. and Timothy Lacey La.
   - (B) Merlin Rd. and Silverdale Rd.
   - (C) Merlin Rd. and Marle Ave.
   - (D) Mary St. and Silverdale Rd.

4. The coordinates for the intersection of Silverdale Rd. and Browns Rd. are _____.

5. The Reserve is between _____ and _____.

6. If I drive in a northerly direction along Montpelier Dr., take the first intersection to the right, then the first to the left, the first street I pass is _____.

7. What are these abbreviations short for?   1. Dr. _____   2. Pl. _____
   3. La. _____   4. Rd. _____   5. St. _____

8. About how far is it from Big Hill Rd. to The Oaks Public School? _____.

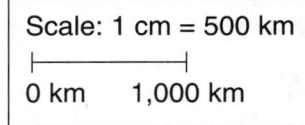
Name: _____   Date: _____

ANTARCTICA

Many countries make territorial claims to parts of Antarctica and several have permanent bases there, but no one has lived there for more than a few years. This map shows the various territorial claims to Antarctic territory and some bases.

Scale: 1 cm = 500 km

├──────┤

0 km   1,000 km

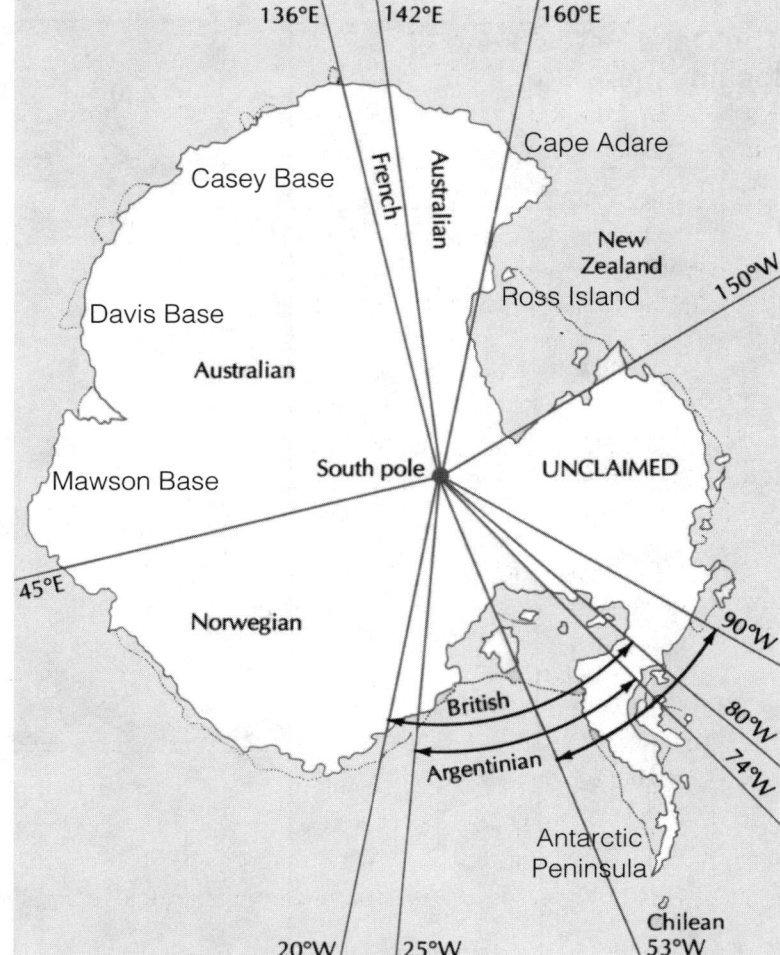

1. How many nations have claims to territory in Antarctica?

_____

2. Which country has two Antarctic claims?

_____

3. What is unusual about the Australian claims?

_____

_____

4. About how far is it from the South Pole to the coast of the Australian territory following the 160° East meridian?

_____

5. Approximately what fraction of Antarctica is unclaimed?

(A) one-sixth

(B) one-fifth

(C) one-third

(D) one-quarter

6. Mt. Erebus is on Ross Island which is part of _____ territory.

7. Which area has three claims on it? The area between

(A) the meridians 25° West and 53° West   (C) the meridians 20° West and 53° West

(B) the meridians 74° West and 80° West   (D) the meridians 53° West and 74° West

8. Which two countries have almost identical claims for the same territory?

_____   _____

9. If I left Davis Base and went in a clockwise direction, the first base I would pass would be the

_____ Base.

Name: _____   Date: _____

INTRODUCTION

Tables, charts, and graphs provide information that has to be read in a particular way. Tables, charts, and graphs require you to understand how the information is presented as well as interpret the information provided. Tables, charts, and graphs are a simple way of providing information without a lot of reading.

In mathematics you may have learned that graphs come in many forms. These include pictographs, bar graphs, column graphs, line graphs, and pie graphs. Information in books is often provided in graph form because it can save lengthy explanations. Most graphs show the relationship between two pieces of information.

These tables from the article "What Authors Get When a Book is Sold" from *Australian Author*, compare how much money an author gets from a sale in a bookshop and from a sale in a book club.

Table 1 — Bookshop Sales What authors get for a book when it is sold in a bookshop MSRP (Manufacturer's Suggested Retail Price) $10.		
	Approx. %	Approx. Proceeds
Bookseller	42%	$4.20
Distributor	18%	$1.80
Publisher	30%	$3.00
Author	10%	$1.00
Total	100%	$10.00

Table 2 — Book Club Sales What authors might receive when a book is sold through a book club (MSRP $10) discount price $8.		
	Approx. %	Approx. Proceeds
Distributor*	70%	$5.60
Publisher	26%	$2.10
Author	4%	$0.30
Total	100%	$8.00

*The book club distribution includes freight, leaflets, client servicing, packing, etc., in a short run turnaround.

1. According to the table, the selling of books through Book Clubs benefits the author more than selling through a bookshop.

   ☐ True   ☐ False

2. In your opinion, which outlet would authors prefer for the distribution of their books?

   _____. What are your reasons? _____

   _____

3. Selling books through book clubs cuts out the need for a _____ .

4. What is the difference in return to the distributor when they sell a $10 book through book clubs

   rather than through a bookshop? $_____

5. How much does the buyer save when buying a $10 book through a book club? $_____

6. The percent return remains much the same for the publisher whether or not the book is sold

   through a bookshop or a book club.   ☐ True   ☐ False

7. Which table shows the best return for the authors?   ☐ Table 1   ☐ Table 2

8. What word in Table 2 indicates that the author's return may be less than 4%? _____

Name: _____   Date: _____

SEASONS AND CLIMATE IN ANTARCTICA

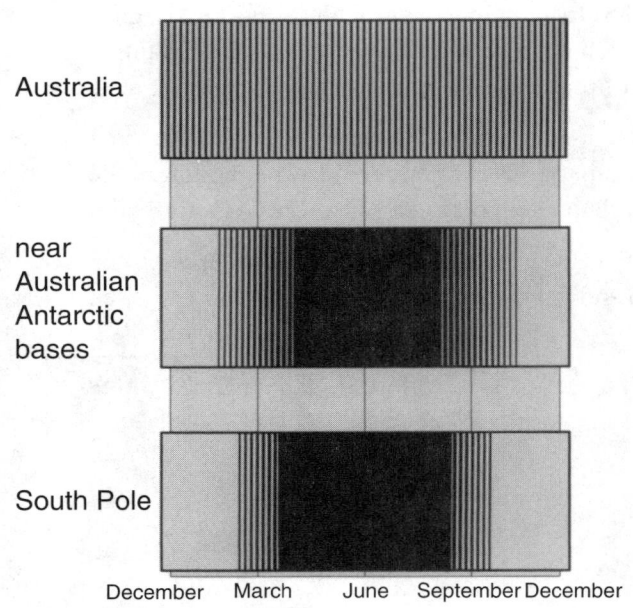

Australia

near Australian Antarctic bases

South Pole

December   March   June   September December

Variations between day and night in different seasons.

		Summer	Winter
Coast	highest	15	−15
	average	0	−20
	lowest (at an Australian base)	−20	−40
Inland	highest	−15	−30
	average	−30	−65
	lowest	−60	−90

Temperatures (°C) in Antarctica

Both charts from *Antarctica* by John Collerson, pp. 14–15

1. Study the two charts and choose the statement which is true.

   (A) The Australian Antarctic base has no night during spring.

   (B) The further south one travels the more daylight there is each year.

   (C) The lowest summer temperature recorded in Antarctica was −90°C.

   (D) The place with the coldest average temperature is inland Antarctica.

2. The _____ area has a temperature above freezing during _____.

3. It is most likely the Australian Antarctic base is situated (Check one answer.)

   ☐ at the South Pole.   ☐ on the Antarctic coast.

4. What is the difference between the average temperature in winter on the coast and the average

   winter temperature inland? _____ °C

5. What is the difference between the highest temperature in summer on the coast and the lowest

   winter temperature inland? _____ °C

6. It is most likely the temperature on the coast

   (A) never rises above zero degrees.

   (B) is quite warm during summer.

   (C) is much the same in summer and winter.

   (D) can fall as low as −40°C during summer.

7. The best season to take an Antarctic scenic flight would be _____ .

ROAD CASUALTIES

Road casualties happen under a number of circumstances. The following graphs show the age distribution of people who become road casualties in a given period.

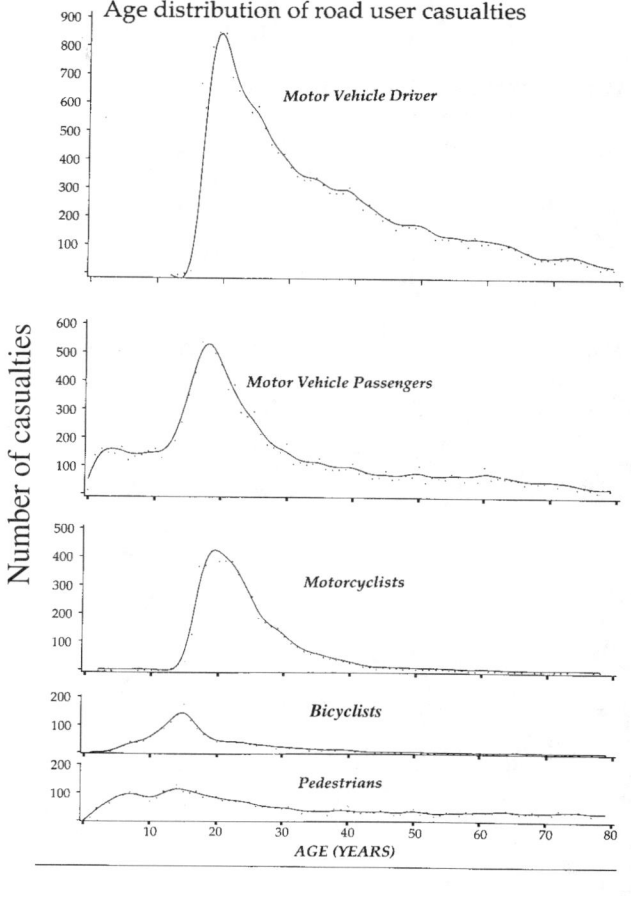

Age distribution of road user casualties

Motor Vehicle Driver

Motor Vehicle Passengers

Motorcyclists

Bicyclists

Pedestrians

Number of casualties

AGE (YEARS)

1. The road users with the lowest casualties are
   (A) vehicle passengers.
   (B) motorcyclists.
   (C) pedestrians.
   (D) bicyclists.

2. Approximately, how many motorcycle casualties are 10 year-olds?
   (A) five
   (B) twenty-five
   (C) fifty
   (D) one hundred

3. Overall, which age group has the most road casualties?
   (A) 5–15 year olds
   (B) 15–25 year olds
   (C) 25–35 year olds
   (D) 35–45 year olds

4. In the pedestrian group, teenagers have the highest casualty rate. ☐ True ☐ False

5. Approximately, how many 20 year-old drivers are involved in road casualties? _____

6. Road casualties hardly change for pedestrians over forty. How would you explain this?

_____

7. Casualties for bicyclists peak with the 15 year-old age group. This may be because
   (A) after 15 children get better quality bicycles.
   (B) as children get older, they move to other methods of travel.
   (C) cyclists over 15 years-old avoid using busy roads.
   (D) drivers become more careful when they see older children cyclists.

8. If you could make a generalization about the information, what would you conclude?

_____

Page 6: Overview—Text Types
1. Suggested answer: William Shakespeare
2. Narrative
3. Tells a story with a start, middle, and end.
4. Suggested answer: Anne Frank
5. Recounts
6. A postcard recounts what is happening in a person's life.
7. Exposition
8. It is an advertisement and the aim is to persuade people.

Page 7: Introduction—Understanding Questions
1. Answers may vary. (Example: Hypnotists have less power than originally thought.)
2. TV show volunteers / are often willing to be hypnotized.
   Research by psychologists / has cast doubt on the popularly held beliefs.
   Hypnotists / are generally believed to have special powers.
3. False
4. the willingness of the volunteer
5. Answers will vary.

Page 8: Freeflyers: Modern Skydivers—Understanding Questions
1. freeflying, greater control is needed
2. 300 km per hour
3. less than one minute
4. creating formations
5. True
6. daring
7. Answers may vary. (They create difficult maneuvers in a group.)
8. sensational
9. conventional
10. False (probably a sports magazine)

Page 9: Cloze Exercises—Understanding Questions
1. (B) but
2. (C) from
3. (D) were
4. (B) huddled
5. (A) avoid
6. (C) displays
7. (B) move
8. with stealth.

Page 10: Circles—Understanding Questions
1. (A) a life of sorrow and desperation.
2. (A) he left home, never expecting to return.
3. (C) something he'd thought he couldn't do.
4. (B) an historical recount.
5. (3) John Costello dies.   (2) The sons dig their mother's grave.
   (4) The narrator began his writing.   (1) Elizabeth Costello leaves her childhood home.

Page 11: Introduction—Finding the Facts
1. frazel ice
2. Most icebergs are found in the Antarctic waters.
3. nine-tenths
4. (D) icebergs
5. plow through pack ice.
6. False

Page 12: Mystery in Mandurah—Finding the Facts
1. getting ready for the crayfishing season.
2. the *Avaneta*
3. (D) an unepected wave swamping the boat.
4. Answers may vary.

5. (B) small fleet.
6. It was claimed the police weren't committed to solving the mystery.

Page 13: The Tree of Life—Finding the Facts
1. (in any order) husk, water, flesh, shell
2. buy picture postcards of them
3. It provides necessities for life—food, fuel, shelter, clothing, household products, and income.
4. False
5. False
6. True
7. long lasting
8. one of the world's great trees.
9. Answers will vary.

Page 14: The Tommy Tycho Story—Finding the Facts
1. Answers may vary: autobiography, narrative, personal recount
2. (C) had only a limited variety of musical experiences.
3. (A) Growing Up with Music
4. True
5. False
6. Answers will vary. (fortunate)
7. distinguished
8. Answers may vary. (successful, fulfilling)
9. Vienna/Budapest (Hungary)

Page 15: Night of the Muttonbirds—Finding the Facts
1. Matthew
2. a younger brother.
3. The late arrival of the plane.
4. agitated
5. (B) the students were all different ages.
6. False
7. the pilot
8. Mr. Trent

Page 16: Our Neighbor in Space—Finding the Facts
1. Answers may vary. (Spring time on Mars)
2. (a) sunlight begins to shine on the ice cap.
   (c) sand dunes are concealed under a frost cover.
   (b) the ice cap has shrunk.
3. False
4. False
5. Mars' ice and snow is formed from carbon dioxide not water.
6. The winds persistently come from the same direction.
7. (B) collect information about the seasons on Mars.

Page 17: Introduction—Finding the Main Idea
1. (C) the provisions of the *National Parks and Wildlife Act of 1974*.
2. (D) obtaining licenses
3. False
4. Native Fauna Regulations
5. Proper care for native Australian animals/Protection for native Australian animals

Page 18: Earth First—Finding the Main Idea
1. The consumption/use of resources has become a concern.
2. luxuries
3. Answers may vary: The practice of using a lot of resources.
4. Commercial packaging is becoming common in developing countries as well as in developed countries.
5. declining
6. in recent decades
7. Answers may vary: An increase in worldwide consumerism has begun to impact our environment.

Page 19: Land of the Rippling Gold—Finding the Main Idea
1. They had looked—and had a dreadful shock.
2. (2) Wendy's mother loses a glove.   (3) The windshield is shattered.
   (1) Wendy's parents have a disagreement.   (4) Edie's face is cut.
3. herself (Wendy)
4. a dressing
5. The Accident
6. True
7. False
8. False
9. Answers may vary. (Wendy—told from her point of view.)

Page 20: Bush Medicine—Finding the Main Idea
1. (B) ridicule doctors who won't accept bush medicines.
2. (A) to release the juices.
3. (B) annoying.
4. (D) healing skin problems.
5. (B) doctors.
6. (C) quiet and apprehensive.
7. Answers may vary. (respect)
8. Answers may vary. (Traditional ways should be respected.)

Page 21: That's a Job for Me!—Finding the Main Idea
1. seven
2. In the world of work, it is easy to be influenced by these fixed concepts and stereotypes.
3. Answers may vary. (Stereotyping/TV/fixed ideas)
4. (B) Men's sports are more exciting to watch than women's sports.
5. Answers may vary. (Things are changing for the better.)
6. Changing Attitudes
7. nobody
8. True
9. Answers will vary.

Page 22: Perfect Timing—Finding the Main Idea
1. Answers may vary. (enjoying the music/excitement at a concert/a great experience/etc.)
2. (A) groups
3. A Stunning Act
4. Once they had finished, they began another of their hits, and then another.
5. False
6. True
7. a collection of songs
8. an enthusiastic
9. Any two of the following: applause, clapping, stamping, whistling, shouting, yelling.

Page 23: Introduction—Making Inferences
1. Answers may vary. (They are looking for a way to break in./They don't want to be seen.)
2. Suggested answers: Nicole and Michael remain calm. They operate without undue discussion. They are not nervous. They know about alarms.
3. With descriptions of trying not to be seen or heard. The reader keeps expecting something to happen.
4. the alarm was set.
5. secretly and quietly
6. They knew how to reach the balcony.

Page 24: The Lady in Black—Making Inferences
1. (D) foreboding.
2. Answers may vary. (detached/somber/industrious)
3. Answers may vary. (threatening/secure, alien/familiar, unknown/known)
4. Brett sees movement in the bushes.
5. (in any order) leeched life, skeletal
6. Answers may vary. (To take passengers to their destination./Complete the journey.)
7. indifference

Page 25: Odious Underarmus, Marathon Man—Making Inferences

1. Answers may vary. (school students)
2. (D) names referring to unpleasant human functions.
3. (A) a comedy.
4. They both relate to fishing. (They are puns.)
5. Answers may vary. (Their names all start with "s." Many are not likely to be fish common to ancient Greece. There is a very wide variety offered. Some of the audience may find some of the fish offered as a little "unacceptable.")
6. (B) a buffoon.
7. promised

Page 26: Politically Correct—Making Inferences

1. pet shop owner
2. Answers will vary.
3. Answers may vary. (He is indifferent to cruelty to animals./He is not very sensitive./He is weary of his job.)
4. pet shop owner
5. (B) angry and appalled
6. Answers may vary. (the ethics of caging birds/cruelty to animals)

Page 27: An Interview with Paul Murphy—Making Inferences

1. (A) a committed broadcaster.
2. sympathetic.
3. That would be the end of his career.
4. cordial.
5. True
6. Answers may vary. (respect/appreciate/feel confident in/value)

Page 28: Book Review—Making Inferences

1. (A) was receptive to the book's style.
2. librarians.
3. (C) one of the first models tested.
4. Dr. Mulder believes Jake's grandfather stole the plans for an electronic game from him.
5. Answers may vary. (evil, sinister, malevolent, revengeful, etc.)
6. consumed by hate
7. Answers will vary.
8. (2) Carson family company is destroyed.
   (1) The plans for an electronic game are stolen.
   (3) At fifteen, Jake is a computer genius and swimming coach.
9. By using real encounters with death.

Page 29: Introduction—Using Context Clues

1. (B) is approaching.
2. Answers may vary. (She didn't want Annabel upset by what might be the truth.)
3. Her face was pressed into Megan's shoulder.
4. Answers may vary. (nervousness/tension/fear/worry)
5. False
6. Answers will vary. (about five) (She is interested in a teddy./She is concerned about the island blowing away.)
7. Answers will vary. (To avoid upsetting Annabel unnecessarily.)

Page 30: The Second Plane—Using Context Clues

1. Suggested answers: taps his ventilator/frowns/forced a smile/couldn't concentrate on his book
2. Bandierante
3. Answers may vary. (relaxed/happy)
4. Answers may vary. (She smiled at Aaron./She is going on vacation looking at tourist leaflet.)
5. vacation plans
6. was reading without thinking about the meaning.
7. True
8. True
9. Answers may vary. (mystery/suspense/adventure)

Page 31: Special Day—Using Context Clues

1. (A) surfing.
2. (D) a long time after the actual event.
3. (A) memorable.
4. (B) time did not matter to the poet.
5. (D) nostalgia.
6. (A) roll about.
7. (B) melancholy
8. Answers will vary. (about 14/15)
9. Answers will vary. (He spends a whole day surfing without parental supervision.)

Page 32: Rugby Union—Using Context Clues

1. impetuous.
2. Answers may vary. (It had an unorthodox beginning. People resist change. The rules didn't seem fair.)
3. (B) Scotland is just across a land border from England.
4. It had its origins at Rugby School.
5. (2) The students at Cambridge begin playing Rugby.
   (1) Ellis disrupts a soccer match by picking up the ball.
   (4) An organization called Rugby Union is formed.
   (3) The new game was called Rugby after the school where Ellis performed his feat.
6. True

Page 33: Introduction—Drawing Conclusions

1. (C) wonderous.
2. Answers may vary. (The number of visitors to Wanaka for the air show/the advice to make hotel reservations well in advance/the number of exhibits at the show)
3. peaceful
4. Wanaka Warplanes
5. There is a wide variety of machinery/vehicle exhibits.
6. False
7. a positive

Page 34: Pudding Recipes—Drawing Conclusions

1. (A) family on camping vacation.
2. Answers will vary. (They most likely originated before modern cooking methods were readily available in the country.)
3. (D) The Billy Can Pudding needs raisins, mixed spice, and cinnamon.
4. (C) be dusted inside with flour.
5. (A) rice, sugar, raisins, and nuts.
6. Answers may vary. (The ingredients have a long shelf life without special storage conditions.)
7. (C) the Australian outback.
8. Answers may vary. (inexpensive, cheap, basic)
9. Billy Can Pudding

Page 35: Tsunami—Drawing Conclusions

1. (C) a falling meteor
2. True
3. reach shallow water, have their origins close to the shore
4. keeping watch
5. False
6. Japanese
7. volcanic explosion, submarine earthquake
8. 1883: Java and Sumatra
9. high

Page 36: The Tattooed Man—Drawing Conclusions
1. Answers will vary.
2. (A) Mel stared at the black panther across the silver bar.
   (C) He could almost see the claws.
3. That he was at the zoo.
4. the dark night, the tattoo, the panther's eyes
5. False
6. the tattooed man
7. The bus grunted forward.

Page 37: Introduction—Noting Details
1. The vast distances and times involved (24 million light years, every 11 million years)
2. appears unremarkable/a typical spiral galaxy
3. a university
4. (C) The speed at which its geysers eject.
5. The speed of the eruptions is much slower.
6. 100 km/sec
7. a more difficult situation
8. moderately
9. spiral

Page 38: Global Warming—Noting Details
1. Ancient: generally of natural cause/happened slowly/rainforests turned to deserts/icecaps expand
   Recent: an increase in greenhouse gases
2. False
3. increasing
4. Industrial Revolution
5. human activity
6. lifestyles
7. floods, droughts
8. use
9. smaller

Page 39: Marauding Elephants Feel the Heat—Noting Details
1. Loki Osborn is developing / a spray to deter elephants.
   Jack Birochak developed / a pepper spray to deter bears.
2. Birochak
3. Cambridge
4. True
5. True
6. False
7. False
8. It deters elephants but is harmless to them.
9. animals
10. grizzly bears
11. keen

Page 40: Introduction—Following Directions
1. two
2. Answers will vary. (about 45 minutes)
3. lightly and quickly beaten
4. drained
5. served warm with a favorite spread
6. measuring spoons, bowls, baking tray, spoon, whisk, knife
7. a brand name for jam

Page 41: Making a Paper Glider—Following Directions

1. instructions (plans, method)
2. 2. Place the paper clips evenly along one of the short sides of the letter-sized paper.
   3. Fold the paper in half.
   4. Fold each side in half again to form the wing.
3. (A) usual.
4. snip
5. materials.
6. To show how to make a paper glider.
7. False

Page 42: Lawn Mower Care Guide—Following Directions

1. (C) exhaust
2. (C) apply oil to improve ease of operaton and control.
3. (A) fuel in tank, clean oil filter, replace worn blades
4. every six months
5. mower owners maintain their machines
6. weekly checks

Page 43: Sausage Recipe—Following Directions

1. Answers may vary. (make the instructions easier to follow/make the package more attractive/make the instructions appear simple)
2. Answers may vary. (a trade name/good old-fashioned quality food)
3. (D) satisfying.
4. (2) Place the ingredients in a dish.   (1) Pierce the sausages.
   (4) Add the creamy recipe mixture.   (3) Prepare the recipe mix.
5. one and a half (1.5)
6. False
7. Answers will vary.
8. Answers may vary.
9. Answers may vary. (traditional, hearty, delicious, creamy, smothered, new)
10. covered

Page 44: Introduction—Understanding Paragraphs

1. a. 1 b. 2 c. 2 d. 2
2. on the open sea
3. on the deck of the launch—the bow
4. there has been a change in speakers.
5. Answer will vary. (Megan. We don't know why she is sitting silently.)
6. moving/feeling
7. Patrick said that he was hungry and asked for something to eat.

Page 45: Mystery in Mandurah—Understanding Paragraphs

1. Yes
2. Answers will vary. (Paragraph 1: when it happened, Paragraph 2: boat fails to meet Jim Spice, Paragraph 3: search failed, Paragraph 4: boat's seaworthiness, Paragraph 5: discovery of equipment, Paragraph 6: floats marked with *Avaneta* number)
3. Answers may vary. (to grab reader's attention/make it quick and easy to read/increase sensationalism)
4. Answers may vary. (Jim Spice said, "I remember the day when I went to meet Gill's vessel, the *Avaneta*, at the government jetty.")
5. discovered/found
6. Answers will vary. (Tragedy at Sea, Local Fishermen Disappear, Town's Great Loss)

Page 46: Paragraph Exercises—Understanding Paragraphs

1.

Patricia Turner was born on December 2, 1939 in Marrickville, Sydney. Her parents were living in New South Wales before she was born. // Soon after Patricia was born, she and her parents moved to an outer suburb of Brisbane. In those days, outer suburbs were more like country towns than urban areas. It was here she came to love the freedom rural life offered. // When she was six, she attended the local primary school. There were less than fifty pupils enrolled at the school in those days, most of them the sons and daughters of local farmers. // Many years later she returned to the school. As she walked in the gate, she could see the changes. More students, more teachers, more buildings. And she was the new principal.

2.

Matthew shifted restlessly in his chair and glanced up at the schoolroom clock on the wall opposite. Ten-thirty already! What had happened? Had something gone wrong? Today was mail day but the plane was later than usual, and on this of all days when his grandmother, Annie, was returning from hospital in Tasmania. In nervous anticipation he sat staring out of the window, chewing his fingernails, listening, waiting. // "Matthew!" Mr. Trent's voice was sharp. // Matthew glanced at him in exasperation, sighed and made a half-hearted attempt to concentrate on the subject in front of him. Then, to his enormous relief, he heard it, at first indistinct but unmistakable. The low steady drone of an aircraft approaching. He stood up pushing his books aside. // "Matthew! Sit down!" // "It's coming," said Matthew. "The plane, I mean. Mr. Greg's coming."

3.

Students threatened with expulsion or suspension from school will now have the opportunity to have their side of the argument heard before a special "education" judge. // The Department of Education has brought in guidelines which will give a student a fair hearing in cases where the student feels he or she has not been treated fairly. // A parent group from the north coast of NSW said that this change was long overdue. // However, groups supporting greater discipline in schools disagree, saying that students now have too many rights and genuine learners are being disadvantaged. // Ms. Kathy Kane, spokesperson for the Department, said she welcomed the change. // The new guidelines will come into effect from the beginning of the new school year.

4.

"I heard that, Michelle!" said Ms. Wright. "Stand up!" // "Who me?" I tried to look innocent. "I didn't say anything!" // Ms. Wright sighed. She looked up at the ceiling then back at me. "It was a ventriloquist, was it?" // I really don't like those sorts of questions. Agree, and you are being rude. Disagree, and you get laughed at by the class.

Page 47: Introduction—Recognizing Persuasion
1. yourself
2. Ride the rapids with Rapid Ride
3. True
4. Families will be more inclined to go on the ride.
5. Yes
6. Answers will vary. (race, exhilarating, blood-pumping, unbelievable, tumbling, etc.)

Page 48: Earth First—Recognizing Persuasion
1. pleasant, wealthy
2. (B) develop consumer/reader awareness.
3. bread
4. Suggested answers: Buy one, get one free. Hurry before time runs out.
5. Answers may vary. (napkins, milk bottles, plastic cups, etc.)
6. Answers will vary.
7. An ideal way of life.

Page 49: The Year 2000 Problem—Recognizing Persuasion

1. (B) more people will be affected than is generally realized.
2. (B) sense of justice.
3. Many machines will recognize 00 as 1900 not 2000.
4. a quick check around the home/kitchen
5. (D) business magazine.
6. fact
7. Time is running out. / Disaster is about to happen.
8. Answers may vary. (The phrase implies that there are many other examples that can be given.)

Page 50: Introduction—Fact or Opinion?

1. strongly approving/biased
2. "I think"
3. opinion
4. opinion
5. fact
6. False
7. Answers may vary. (The poor reporting of important events—wars—on the news.)

Page 51: Shopping Carts—Fact or Opinion?

1. Poor supervision by parents may be as much to blame for the accidents. / Children should ride in a separate carrier.
2. True
3. A separate survey has shown that 80% of parents leave their child unattended. / They [pediatricians] think the child should be closer to the ground. (*Note:* It is a <u>fact</u> that the pediatricians hold this <u>opinion</u>.) / The child's seat, located high on the cart, gives the cart a high center of gravity.
4. think, suggest
5. False
6. Answers will vary. (like, believe, accept)
7. True

Page 52: Global Warming—Fact or Opinion?

1. (C) The way we communicate and even our health may be affected.
2. fact
3. No.
4. Answers will vary. (It's too speculative. / It is an ongoing event rather than new. / The text is too dense for front page.)
5. False
6. (C) with the start of the Industrial Revolution.
7. Animals do not use technology.

Page 53: Introduction—Relevant and Irrelevant Information

1. Sometimes the counters are called "men."
2. (B) From Wanaka, snow-capped mountains can be seen.
3. the size of the crowd
4. False
5. False

Page 54: Taking Better Photos—Relevant and Irrelevant Information

1. Even in non-flash photos, many photographers stand too far away from their subjects.
2. it is an action shot.
3. (D) Making sure the room is as light as possible.
4. At least two meters.
5. Answers may vary. (To pre-focus the camera)
6. Answers will vary.
7. False

Page 55: Introduction—Understanding and Using a Table of Contents
1. pages 28 and 29
2. True
3. Chapter 1 "Feelings"
4. glossary
5. pages 24 and 25
6. index
7. "sensitivity"

Page 56: The Age of Dinosaurs in Australia—Understanding and Using a Table of Contents
1. page 34
2. Finding and Studying Dinosaurs
3. Suggested Reading or Bibliography
4. Index
5. False
6. False
7. True
8. Australia
9. The Age of Dinosaurs in Australia

Page 57: Introduction—Understanding and Using an Index
1. pages 40 and 41
2. two (40 to 46 and 48)
3. recycling
4. eight
5. climate
6. electricity/nuclear energy/fossil fuels
7. 19
8. soil

Page 58: Shaping the News—Understanding and Using an Index
1. page 6
2. an illustration
3. 25
4. Cave (Peter)
5. alphabetical order.
6. False
7. True
8. Answers may vary. (Radio has more pages of information than crime.)
9. are two

Page 59: Introduction—Using Schedules
1. WBN
2. 1 hr. 25 min.
3. No
4. WBN
5. Parent guidance (recommended)
6. 8:30 P.M.
7. the movie <u>Comet</u>
8. No
9. True
10. False
11. 4 hrs. 50 min.
12. Sports Scene
13. nothing (free)
14. WSB
15. <u>Comet</u>

ANSWER KEY

Page 60: Bega Valley Mobile Library Service—Using Schedules
1. Tuesday
2. (D) in alphabetical order of the communities.
3. (A) the number of visits it has each month
4. (in any order) Pambula, Tathra, Wyndham
5. 6 hours
6. public holiday
7. True
8. Wyndham

Page 61: Introduction—Reading Maps
1. (C) northeast
2. (D) F 10.
3. (A) Silverdale Rd. and Timothy Lacey La.
4. G 6
5. (in any order) William St. and Monkey Creek
6. Cedar Pl.
7. Drive, Place, Lane, Road, Street
8. About 2 km

Page 62: Antarctica—Reading Maps
1. seven
2. Australia
3. It is divided by a small French claim.
4. 1,000 km
5. (A) one-sixth
6. New Zealand
7. (D) the meridians 53° West and 74° West
8. Argentina and Britain
9. Casey

Page 63: Introduction—Interpreting Tables, Charts, and Graphs
1. False
2. Bookshops. Higher returns per book.
3. bookseller
4. $3.80
5. $2.00
6. False
7. Table 1
8. "might"

Page 64: Seasons and Climate in Antarctica—Interpreting Tables, Charts, and Graphs
1. (D) The place with the coldest average temperature is inland Antarctica.
2. coastal, summer
3. on the Antarctic coast.
4. 45°C
5. 105°C
6. (B) is quite warm during summer.
7. summer

Page 65: Road Casualties—Interpreting Tables, Charts, and Graphs
1. (D) bicyclists.
2. (A) five
3. (B) 15–25 year olds
4. True
5. 850
6. Answers may vary. (Older people don't walk as often. / Older people are more careful when crossing.)
7. (B) as children get older, they move to other methods of travel.
8. Answers will vary. (Driving a car is the most dangerous form of transport. / People become more careful road users as they get older.)

Name: _____   Date: _____

THE NEWSROOM

Use this concept wheel to help you **find facts** so you can visualize information, thoughts, and ideas. Read an article or passage and use this organizer to answer the questions *who, what, where, why, when,* and *how.*

Headline:

Byline:	Dateline:
Who?	What?
Where?	Why?
When?	How?

Name: _____   Date: _____

WEB PLUS SUBS

Read your article or passage. **Find the main idea or topic** and write it in the middle. Then find the subheadings and write those in the outer circles. Then write the supporting details to those subheadings.

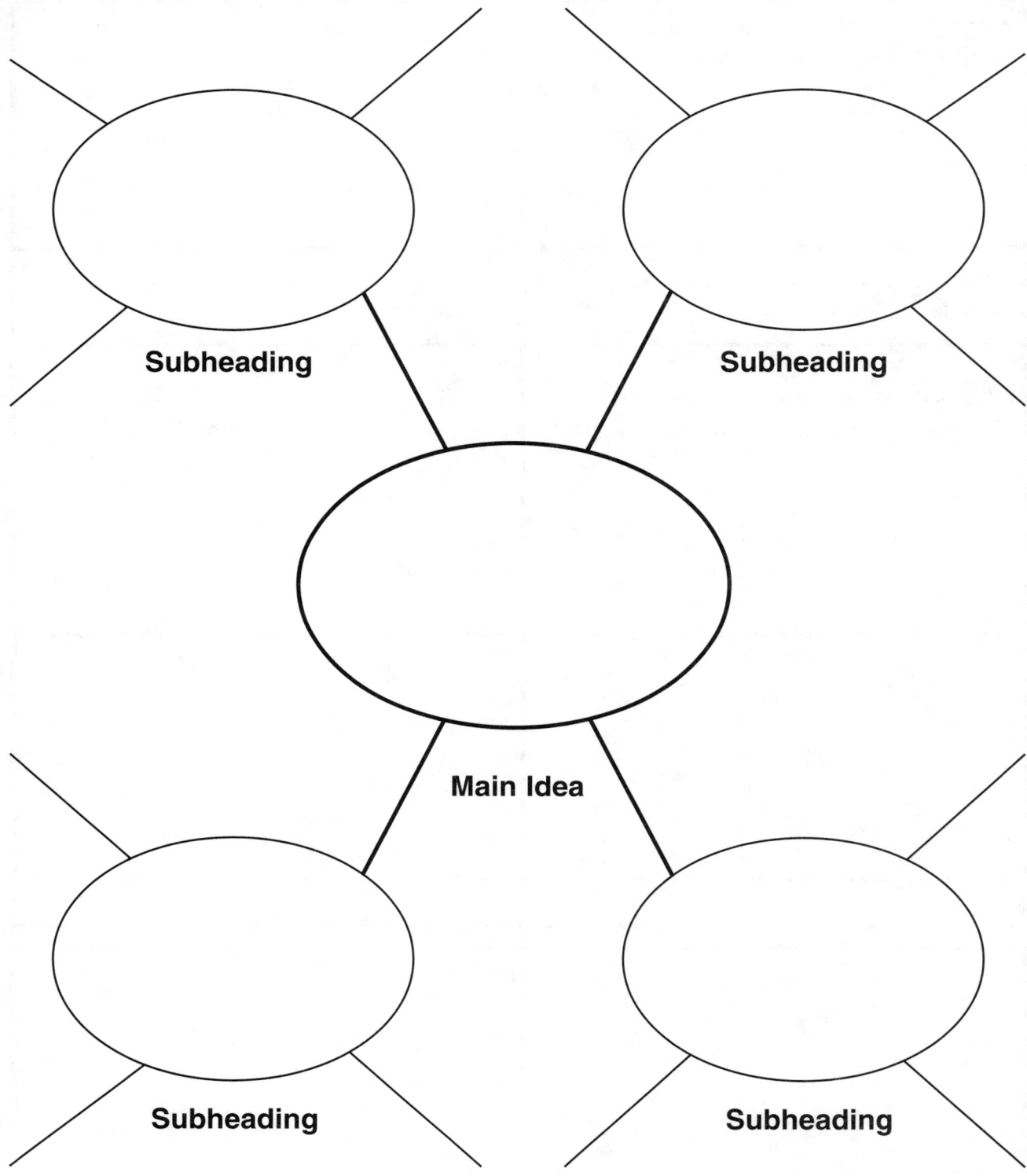

Subheading

Subheading

Main Idea

Subheading

Subheading

FIVE-PARAGRAPH ESSAY

Use this web to organize your thoughts and help you **understand paragraphs**. Write down the main topic of the article or passage. Then read each paragraph and write the supporting topic and all the details. Then write a conclusion.

Main Idea, Introductory, and Thesis Paragraph

Support/Proof Details

Support/Proof Details

Support/Proof Details

Summary/Conclusion

Name: _____   Date: _____

OUTLINING

Use this web to organize your thoughts and help you **understand paragraphs**. Write down the main topic of the article or passage. Then read each paragraph and write all the details. Then write a conclusion.

Title: [   ]

I. Introductory Paragraph

    A.

    B.

    C.

II. Supporting Body Paragraph

    A.

    B.

    C.

III. Supporting Body Paragraph

    A.

    B.

    C.

IV. Supporting Body Paragraph

    A.

    B.

    C.

V. Concluding Paragraph

    A.

    B.

    C.